LIVING IN BONDAGE OF SPIRITUAL FEAR OF THE UNKNOWN

–

A DEBILITATING ENSLAVEMENT OF THE MIND

LIVING IN BONDAGE OF SPIRITUAL FEAR OF THE UNKNOWN –

A DEBILITATING ENSLAVEMENT OF THE MIND

DR. EMEKA O. OZURUMBA

Printed in the United States of America.

First Edition 2017

To order additional copies of this book, contact:

Today Evangelical Ministries, Inc.
713-297-1498; 713-484-5600;
www.temonline.org

CONTENTS

DEDICATION

To the exclusive glory of God.

PREFACE

This book is a wake-up call to all those who are wallowing in bondage of spiritual fear of the unknown and the ever-pressing weight and strongholds of false prophets and deliverers, to redeem the time and shake off the shackles of slavery. Whoever is brought to bondage of fear of the unknown is certainly a slave – a slave of his lord (devil or man), for he neither has liberty nor sound mind. The apostle Peter wrote concerning destructive deeds of false prophets, thus: "While they promise them liberty, they themselves are slaves of corruption; for by whom a person is overcome, by him also he is brought into bondage" (2 Peter 2:19). The scripture says that fear has a stinging torment, and whoever is spiritually fearful is not perfect in God – for where the Spirit of God is there is freedom and liberty (see 2 Cor. 3:17; 1 John 4:18). The greatest battles are waged in our mind, and whatever or whoever controls our mind has effectively overcome us. It is, therefore, incumbent on all those who are victimized by spiritual fear of the unknown to wake from slumber and depression and cling to the knowledge and understanding of the truth revealed in this book for their freedom from bondage. As it is written by apostle Paul to the Ephesians: "Awake, you who sleep, arise from the dead, and Christ will give you light. "See then that you walk circumspectly, not as fools but as wise, redeeming the time, because the days are evil, "Therefore do not be unwise, but understand what the will of the Lord [not the will of man] is" (Eph. 5:14-17).

The will of God for us is to perfect the fear of Him (depart, forsake, hate and abhor all evil/sinful ways), and abide fully in every word of His only begotten Son, Jesus Christ (hear only His voice, not confusing voices of wicked men and the evil spirits they serve); for God manifested Himself to us by His Son, so that we have no more excuse if we continue to go astray and invite deceivers to control and exploit us (see Deut. 5:29, 10:12-13; John 1:1-5, 3:16, 10:27-28, 14:6, 15:7, 22; Rom. 1:17-20; Heb.1:1-4).

The reader must know and accept the fact that there is no amount of rituals that can deliver or liberate a soul, family or land from the menacing attacks of demons; spiritual fear is neither hereditary nor as a result of generational curse; and our merciful God never commanded generational curse, as a general rule. Therefore, henceforth, whoever desires to be free from spiritual fear and "overwhelming giants" must reject all false prophets and fake deliverers and liberators, and strive at all cost to know the truth in Christ, by living and being the truth, anchored on the solid foundation of

Christ (fear of the Lord, which is to depart from all iniquities). This is the only way to pull and cast down all strongholds, arguments and everything in us which mitigates against our knowledge of God, for His full armor of protection against the attacks of the enemy.

It is my sincere hope that this book will not be read as a condemnation of ministers of the Gospel of Christ. That will be far from the truth and intent of this book; for there are many faithful servants of the Lord, who must be respected and commended; but the many rotten elements in the so-called body of Christ have eroded respect and confidence in an institution (church), which is expected to be a beacon of light, hope, morality, liberty and love for all. Rather the book is a wake-up call for all of us to repent of our wicked and deceitful ways and return God's children to His undiluted truth of life so that none perishes. My joy will be full in the Lord if this book succeeds in setting a single soul free from the bondage of spiritual fear, and manipulative, deceptive and lying strongholds of men. Since the book is not written for any earthly gain, it is my prayer that God will raise sponsors to cause it (book) to reach every reader without charge. However, if any minister is offended, he is convicted of his own wrong, for the truth of God judges and condemns those who insult His Spirit of truth; and those who scatter and destroy God's flock are His enemies, who must be stopped (see Jer. 12:10, 23:1-2; Ezek. 34: 1-10; Matt. 5:19, 12:37, 18: 6-9, 23:13-14; John 3:19, 12: 47-48; 2 Tim. 3:16; Titus 1:11; 2 Pet. 2:1-3).

ACKNOWLEDGEMENT

I owe great gratitude and debt to many wonderful and supportive people who encouraged, helped and supported me during the writing and preparation of the manuscript. The book owes its existence to a great number of people, specifically and especially, all faithful members of Today Evangelical Ministries, Houston, Texas, U.S. A., for their family love, commitment and dedication to God's undiluted truth, and the effectual dissemination of same all over the world; my beloved wife, Ugochi K. Ozurumba, for her unyielding love, support, encouragement and understanding; Pastor Charles Adiukwu, who tirelessly typed and reviewed the manuscript; Pastor Ifeanyi Akamelu, for countless hours he spent in typing the manuscript; Pastor Godwin Uchegbu and sisters Anthonia Uduma, Olo Abubakar, and Lape Ogunrinde, for their special encouragement and reminder throughout the course of this project; Emeka Emmanuel Anekwe, MD, and Adekunle Adedeji, MD, for their selfless support, assistance and encouragement, I am humbly grateful and appreciative. May the Lord establish and enrich your knowledge and understanding of Him, to the intent that you may be perfect in your walk with Him, who has called us to be wholly conformed to His image and glory.

LIVING IN BONDAGE OF SPIRITUAL FEAR OF THE UNKNOWN –

A DEBILITATING ENSLAVEMENT OF THE MIND

INTRODUCTION

With profound gratitude and humility, I give God all exclusive glory for inspiring, ordaining and completing the writing of this book, the sole purpose of which is the urgent divine deliverance of millions of His children from the crushing weight of bondage of spiritual fear of the unknown, and the manipulative, deceptive, and lying strongholds of agents of darkness (men and women), parading themselves as ministers of the Gospel of Jesus Christ. I thankfully and joyfully herald God's outstretched hands to intervene and set His children free from this evil monstrous foe, which chokes and strangulates its victims with its ever-debilitating enslavement of their mind. As it is written: "He [God] saw that there was no man, and wondered that there was no intercessor; therefore, His own arm brought salvation for Him; and His own righteousness, it sustained Him" (Is. 59:16). I strongly believe this book is a strong tool in His arm to bring salvation and redemption to His victimized, tormented and abused children.

Alarmingly, the greatest hindrance to spiritual growth for Christians in most developing world, like Africa, is the ever-domineering spiritual fear of powers of unknown forces. Most Christians in these infected nations are either walking dead or paralyzed and robbed of their identity within their own prisons without walls. Abominably, this devastating evil (spiritual fear) has now become the principal tool of choice in the hands of "feel good," prosperity, false prophets/prophetess and preachers for effectuation of their wicked and evil enterprise – to make merchandise of, destroy and kill gullible and vulnerable children of God.

These false and fake deliverers and liberators are destroyers of God's vineyard and enemies of the Cross, within the body of Christ – whose specialty is to initiate, reinforce, and perpetuate bondage of fear for their covetous gain, rather than set the captive free. As it is written in the Book of Jeremiah: "Because from the least of them even to the greatest, everyone is given to covetousness; and from the prophet even to the priest, everyone deals falsely" (Jer. 6:13). The Lord abhors abominations of agents of darkness, and commands us to reject, denounce, reprove, correct and expose them (see Matt. 24:24-27; Eph. 5:6-11; 1 Tim. 6:3-5; 2 Tim. 3:1-7, 13, 16-17, 4:1-4; 2 John 1:9-11).

The book is riddled with blunt and uncompromising truth in Christ, in deference to the Spirit of God, for the pulling down of strongholds, and breaking of the evil yoke of bondage. The contexts are strictly based on spiritual revelations, personal counselor experiences and encounters, and indisputable and verifiable facts of the prevailing bondage of spiritual fear, fueled by devouring wolves in sheep clothing. The first ten chapters of the book concisely and precisely discuss the existence and reality of demons and demonic attacks, the unreasonableness of spiritual fear of the unknown, and what it means to be born again of the Spirit of God; lessons from the Book of Job – God will never forsake His own, and none can snatch His out of His hands, the "IF" factor of our relationship with God; the origin of spiritual fear, there is no generational curse, the sad state of a community in bondage, and pathetic testimonies of enslaved minds in the land of freedom and liberty. The other ten chapters discuss the devastating consequences of spiritual fear, and how to eliminate gullibility and vulnerability with the two keys of the kingdom of God; beware of false prophets, and avoid worthless liberation and deliverance rituals; the mystery of mysteries which overcomes all overwhelming fear and 'giants', understanding the place of prayers and vigils, and fighting a successful spiritual warfare – orders of spiritual warfare, which is a must read for all.

The reader must take notice of a few scriptures which are referenced and/or cited in more than one chapter. This is deliberate on the part of the author to ensure clarity, relevance, emphasis, and chapter independence – thereby making each chapter to stand on its own, as to be profitable for instruction, correction, and reproof, when and to the extent it is necessary.

It is equally worthy of notice that all authority referenced and cited in this book is exclusively from the Holy Bible, the only infallible authority and word of God. Since all discussions and conclusions of the author are scripturally based, it is therefore imperatively prudent for the reader to arm himself/herself with the Holy Bible, while reading this book.

CHAPTER ONE

EXISTENCE AND REALITY OF DEMONS AND DEMONIC ATTACK

The devil – that evil spirit, which is referenced by many names, such as Satan, demon, enemy, liar, deceiver, adversary, accuser, prince of darkness, murderer, principality – to just mention but a few, exists. It is certainly prudent for Christians to take spiritual notice and acceptance of the existence and reality of demons and their often potently devastating and tormenting attacks, especially against God's elect. The Holy Bible, the authoritative and infallible word of God, says that demons and demonic attacks abound. For the avoidance of any misunderstanding or misconstruction of my position and to dispel any accusation of naivety on my part, let me clearly say that from the totality of biblical references, buttressed by counselor and personal experiences, I too believe and affirm the existence and reality of demons and their menacing attacks. There is hardly any book of the Holy Bible that falls short of references to the

1

devil and his destructive attacks and devices. To substantiate this belief/conclusion, it is only proper to cite and refer to some prominent mention of demons and their evil attacks and assaults against the authority and domain of God and His children. The fall of the first man [Adam] was directly credited to the devil; our Lord and Savior Jesus Christ was tempted by the devil, and even the book of the Revelation of Jesus Christ contains descriptively detailed accounts of the devil's relentless war against the children of God. As it is written: And the Lord said to the woman [Eve], "What is this you have done?" The woman said, "The serpent [devil] deceived me, and I ate" (Gen. 3:13). Again, "Then he [devil] opened his mouth in blasphemy against God to blaspheme His name, His tabernacle and those who dwell in heaven." "It was granted to him to make war with the saints and to overcome them. And authority was given him over every tribe, tongue, and nation. All who dwell on the earth will worship him, whose names have not been written in the Book of Life of the Lamb slain from the foundation of the world" (Rev. 13:6-8).

The first chapter of the Book of Job tells us of an interesting dialogue between God and Satan relative to Job: "Now there was a day when the sons of God came to present themselves before the LORD, and Satan also came among them. And the LORD said to Satan, "From where do you come?" So Satan answered the LORD and said, "From going to and fro on the earth, and from walking back and forth on it" (Job 1:6-7). Your informed assumption may be as good as mine as to Satan's purpose of wandering around the earth. For the apostle Peter warned us to always be sober and at alert, because the devil walks about like a roaring lion, seeking whom he may devour (see 1 Peter 5:8). But one wonders aloud who the devil is seeking to devour? The answer is obvious – anyone – since he had the guts to tempt our Lord and Savior, Jesus Christ. But as for whom he may succeed in devouring, the answer also appears obvious – his own, that is the one whose fence is broken - the one who gives him room or invites him – that is, the one who has something of the devil in him. Incidentally, Satan was unable to attack Job, because Job had the whole hedge (armor) of God around him; and the reason Job had such impenetrable hedge around him is because, as it is written: "There was a man in the land of Uz, whose name was Job; and that man was blameless and upright, and one who feared God and shunned evil" (Job 1:1).

The book of Zechariah records that Joshua, the high priest of the Lord, was being opposed by Satan, even though he [Joshua] was standing before the angel of the Lord. Joshua, as we read, had filthy garments in his heart, and for that reason, he made Satan an invitee, who opposed him until the filthy garments were taken away from him. "Then he showed me Joshua the high priest standing before the Angel of the LORD, and Satan standing at his right hand to oppose him. And the LORD said to Satan, "The LORD rebuke you, Satan! The LORD who has chosen Jerusalem rebuke you! Is this not a brand plucked from the fire?" Now Joshua was clothed with filthy garments and was standing before the Angel. Then He answered and spoke to those who stood before Him, saying, "Take away the filthy garments from him." And to him, He said, "See, I have removed your iniquity from you, and I will clothe you with rich robes" (Zech. 3:1-4). It is noteworthy that although Joshua was a 'brand plucked (refined) from the fire', by wearing filthy garments (iniquities), he extended an invitation to the devil to oppose him.

The manifest boldness, destructive and derailing tactics of Satan were amplified in his brazen temptation of the Lord, Jesus Christ. It is even more noteworthy that although Christ is the only begotten Son of God, and head of all principality, yet Satan still made all attempts to derail God's mission. As it is written: "Then Jesus was led up by the Spirit into the wilderness to be tempted by the devil. And when He had fasted forty days and forty nights, afterward He was hungry. Now when the tempter came to Him, he said, "If You are the Son of God, command that these stones become bread" (Matt. 4:1-3). The temptation of our Lord is a clear evidence that the devil does not only attack those who are saddled with filthy garments but rather no one is immune from demonic attacks. It further demonstrates that although Satan may attack anyone, only those who have wholly put on Christ (whole/full armor of God) can withstand and overcome him.

And who have put on Christ? - but (only) those who implicitly abide in His words, for these are His true disciples

– He has become Lord for them; and as such none can harm them (see John 8:31, 15:14, 16:33; Gal. 3:27; 1 Pet. 3:13).

Many of the Lord's healing miracles were casting out demons and cutting off occasions of his vicious attacks, among them included, but not limited to, the demon possessed man in a Capernaum synagogue (Mark 1:20-26), a demon possessed blind and mute man (Matt. 12:22), the two demon possessed men of Gadarene (Matt. 8:28) and the lunatic child (Matt. 17:14-18). The Lord even talked about a woman who was bound for eighteen years by Satan. "So ought not this woman, being a daughter of Abraham, whom Satan has bound [think of it] for eighteen years, be loosed from this bond on the Sabbath?" (Luke 13:16). Likewise, all the apostolic epistles made numerous references to demons and demonic attacks; and the Revelation of Jesus Christ, the last book of the Holy Bible, centers on Satan and his agents opposing and waging relentless wars against the children of the kingdom of God.

Now that a sketchy, but biblically conclusive fact has been established of the existence of demons and demonic attacks, I must equally and conclusively state that it remains true that spiritual fear of the unknown is unjustified and shouldn't have any significance in the life of those who are truly born of the Spirit of God. For an enlightening answer to the challenging issue of spiritual fear of the unknown, we turn to the next chapter.

Dr. Emeka O. Ozurumba

CHAPTER TWO

UNREASONABLENESS OF SPIRITUAL FEAR OF THE UNKNOWN AND DEMONIC ATTACKS

The facts and circumstances enumerated in the preceding chapter are reasonably conclusive of the obvious truth and reality of the existence of demons and their demonic attacks and torments. Spiritual attacks, therefore are real, and they are more frequently unleashed against true children of God. As it is written: "For we do not wrestle against flesh and blood, but against principalities, against powers, against the rulers of the darkness of this age, against spiritual hosts of wickedness in the heavenly places" (Eph. 6:12). As it has been from the beginning, the world of darkness and its ruler (Satan) will ceaselessly hunt for the demise of the upright – always seeking/trying to devour, steal, kill and destroy the good (see John 10:10). As we are rightly cautioned by the

7

apostle Peter, "Be sober, be vigilant; because your adversary the devil walks about like a roaring lion, seeking whom he may devour." (1 Pet. 5:8). The apostle Paul pointedly reminded us that the evil one will always seek to derail, distract, torment and destroy the good. "But, as he who was born according to the flesh then persecuted him who was born according to the Spirit, even so, it is now." (Gal. 4:29).

In chapter seventeen of the gospel according to John, the Lord prayed to the Father to keep His apostles from the evil one. As it is written: "I have given them Your word; and the world has hated them because they are not of the world, just as I am not of the world. I do not pray that You should take them out of the world, but that You should keep them from the evil one" (John 17:14-15).

Nevertheless, while the existence and reality of demons and their menacing attacks are conclusively incontrovertible, the scriptures firmly adjudge that the fear of demonic attacks is uncharacteristic of God and therefore un-Christ-like; because spiritual fear is a form of bondage, devoid of liberty; it is unrealistically illogical and self-defeating for all those who profess to be truly born again of the Spirit of God. One who is spiritually fearful of the UNKNOWN is still in darkness, not knowing his way; and is yet to be delivered from the fear of death and transformed into the image of Christ. Those who are born of the Spirit of God are those who have been delivered from the power of darkness and fear of death, transformed into His light. This is a simple and correct definition of salvation. As it is written: "He has delivered us from the power of darkness and conveyed [transformed/translated/transferred] us into the kingdom of the Son of His love," (Col. 1:13). Again: "Inasmuch then as the children have partaken of flesh and blood, He Himself likewise shared in the same, that through death He might destroy him who had the power of death, that is, the devil, and release those who through fear of death were all their lifetime subject to bondage" (Heb. 2:14-15).

If those who claim to be born of God are not the light that overcomes darkness, they are certainly in darkness. For it is written: "This is the message which we have heard from Him and declare to you, that God is light and in Him is no darkness at all. If we say that we have fellowship with Him, and walk in darkness, we lie and do not practice the truth. But if we walk in the light as He is in the light, we have fellowship with one another, and the blood of Jesus Christ His Son cleanses us from all sin" (1 John 1:5-7).

One who is born of God has not only the mind of Christ; but also has the mind that is in Christ, which mind is spiritual – a mind set on heaven, far above all principalities and powers of darkness. As it is written: "But the natural man does not receive the things of the Spirit of God, for they are foolishness to him; nor can he know them, because they are spiritually discerned. But he who is spiritual judges all things, yet he himself is rightly judged by no one. For "WHO HAS KNOWN THE MIND OF THE LORD THAT HE MAY INSTRUCT HIM?" But we have the mind of Christ" (1 Cor. 2:14-16). One who is spiritually fearful lacks one of the essential characteristics of a child of God – spiritual mind; he is yet to be a complete new creation of God (see 2 Cor. 5:17); for he is still wallowing in the futility of his mind, as a

9

gentile (unbeliever). One who possesses characteristics of unbelievers is an unbeliever. One who is born of God must necessarily have a spiritual mind that is renewed all the time, a mind (like the mind of Christ) raised with Christ and set on things above, where Christ is seated at the right hand of the Majesty. As the apostle Paul wrote in his letter to the Ephesians, "This I say, therefore, and testify in the Lord, that you should no longer walk as the rest of the Gentiles walk, in the futility of their mind," "and be renewed in the spirit of your mind" (Eph. 4:17, 23).

The preceding paragraph clearly states that those who are born of God must possess spiritual mind – not enslaved mind. It is evident that the apostle Paul's epistle to the Ephesians was addressed to those "saints" who were born again of God. As he wrote to them, "…that you put off, concerning your former conduct, the old man which grows corrupt according to the deceitful lusts, and be renewed in the spirit of your mind, and that you put on the new man which was created according to God, in true righteousness and holiness" (Eph. 4:22-24).

It certainly is obvious that only a spirit possesses a spiritual mind and this is so, since those who are truly born again of God are spirits of God, and as such gods to the unbelieving world and the prince of this world (see John 3:5-6). For more in-depth on what it means to be truly born again (transformed and regenerated into His image), we turn to the next chapter.

CHAPTER THREE

UNDERSTANDING WHAT IT MEANS TO BE BORN OF GOD (BORN AGAIN)

Simply put, total transformation or regeneration, or conformation to the image of God and His Christ is the sole reason God sent His only begotten Son; needless to say that it is the only purpose of God for us, according to His election; Jesus Christ being the amazing grace of God who came down from heaven to teach (show) us the only way to God – the narrow and straight highway of righteousness and holiness – the highway of eternal life (see Is. 35:8-9; Matt. 7:13-14; Titus 2:11-14). "And we know that all things work together for good to those who love God, to those who are the called according to His purpose" (Rom. 8:28). And what is that purpose? "For whom He foreknew, He also predestined to be conformed to the image of His Son, that He might be the firstborn among many brethren" (Rom. 8:29). God so loved us that He had mercy; mercy begets

11

grace, grace begets spiritual repentance, spiritual repentance begets implicit obedience, and implicit (perfect/complete) obedience begets righteousness and holiness – which is total transformation to His image, or true knowledge of God, which is eternal life (see John 14:6, John 17:3; Rom. 2:4, Rom.6:15, 9:15; 1 John 2:3-5). This is a divine formula: Love -> Mercy-> Grace -> Repentance (Perfection of the fear of God – to depart from all evil deeds) -> Obedience -> Righteousness and holiness (transformation / born again of God) = eternal life.

Grace, therefore, is an unmerited favor given to us to fulfill the sole purpose of our creation and calling – regeneration to His image. A life that does not fulfill this sole purpose is a wasted one. Hence grace is God's goodness which leads to true repentance (see Rom. 2:4). And repentance is invalid except it fulfills the perfection of the fear of God – which is to depart from or forsake all evil/sinful ways, and never returning to the same vomit. As it is written: "Therefore, leaving the discussion of the elementary principles of Christ, let us go on to perfection, not laying again the foundation of repentance from dead works and of faith toward God" (Heb. 6:1). In other words, true repentance is a vow not to repent again of the same sins which ruled us while we were in ignorance. Hence, the Lord admonished the woman caught in adultery to go and sin no more (see John 8:11). As it is written: "For godly sorrow worketh repentance to salvation not to be repented of: but the sorrow of the world worketh death." (2 Cor. 7:10 KJV).

Therefore, one who is born of God does not intentionally, willingly, knowingly, or recklessly put on filthy garments or return to their vomit. For one who returns to his vomit is a fool, who does not know God (see Prov. 26:11).

One who is born of God must be a spirit of His, and if of the Spirit of God, it holds true that he is god - a complete replica of God, fused together in spiritual agreement with Him (see John 3:5-6; 1 John 1:5-7, 2:6, 3:3, 4:17). For two, it is written, cannot walk together except they are in complete agreement (see Amos 3:3). It, therefore, holds true that one who is born of God has put on God, with all His spiritual characteristics – spiritual heart (heart of love, compassion and obedience), spiritual mind (a sound mind which is set above), spiritual body (the holiest temple where God dwells and a new spirit (the Spirit of Christ). When we are in total agreement with God through perfect love and implicit obedience, His Spirit abides in us, and as such, the kingdom of God being within us, we become gods to unbelievers, and even demons and principalities are made subject to us. That is the same authority our Lord gave to His true followers/disciples (those who abide in His word and His word abides in them), thus: "Behold, I give you the authority to trample on serpents and scorpions, and over [ALL] the power of the enemy and nothing shall by any means hurt you" (Luke 10:19). However, there is a caveat to that authority – the "IF" factor. Hence, the Lord cautioned His disciples of the most important exigent thing, and indeed, the only way for the authority to profit them is to ensure that their names are written in heaven (see Luke 10:20). This is analogous with God's instructions to His servant in chapter one of the Book of Joshua. There, God assured Joshua that no man or demon should be able to stand before him all the days of his life, because He, (God) would be with him, and

God would be with Joshua if, and only if, he observed to do all He had commanded him to do. In other words, nothing could stand before Joshua if he was one with God through implicit obedience (see Joshua 1:5-8). One who is spiritually fearful of demons or the UNKNOWN is not perfect in God (love and obedience), and therefore yet to be born again of God. As it is written: "There is no fear in love, but perfect love casts out fear because fear involves torment. But he who fears has not been made perfect in love" (1 John 4:18). One who is spiritually fearful of the UNKNOWN is yet in bondage, for the Spirit of God is not in him; for where the Spirit of God is, there is liberty (see 2 Cor. 3:17). Again, it is written: "But you are not in the flesh but in the Spirit, if indeed the Spirit of God dwells in you. Now if anyone does not have the Spirit of Christ, he is not His" (Rom. 8:9).

Those who are truly born of the Spirit of God have the Spirit of God and are of sound mind; they also possess authority over demons (see Luke 9:1, 10:19). I must say, that spiritual fear of demons or demonic attacks or the UNKNOWN simply abdicates that power and authority. As it is written: "For God has not given us a spirit of fear, but of power and of love and of a sound mind." (2 Tim. 1:7) As a further way of enlightenment and encouragement, we turn to the next chapter to review the lessons from Job, as a case study.

CHAPTER FOUR

THE LESSONS FROM THE BOOK OF JOB
– A CASE STUDY

If there be any consolation, and /or encouragement, the following relevant lessons emerge from the first chapter of the Book of Job, which lessons are set as an example, and written for our understanding. In that chapter, we read that the devil couldn't touch Job because he (Job) had God's full hedge (whole armor) around him and his family. We also read that God had His hedge around Job because Job was one with God through implicit obedience to every commandment of God. Referring to Job, the scripture testifies that "There was a man in the land of Uz, whose name was Job; and that man was blameless and upright, and one who feared God and shunned evil." (Job 1:1). Job had divine understanding which we must all strive to get – the only way to walk together with God is to implicitly obey Him and shun all evil/sinful ways. Frankly, implicit obedience to God's words or commandments is the only way we show our love for, knowledge of, appreciation of, and reverence to Him. As he (Job) later stated: "And to man, He said, 'Behold, the fear of the Lord, that is wisdom, And to depart from evil is understanding' " (Job 28:28).

The second lesson is that the only way to resist the enemy or have power and authority over him is to put on the full hedge/armor of God before the enemy even tries to attack. Hear Satan's frustration because he was rendered powerless to touch Job. "So Satan answered the LORD and said, "Does Job fear God for nothing? Have You not made a hedge around him, around his household, and around all that he has on every side? You have blessed the work of his hands, and his possessions have increased in the land" (Job 1:9-10). Ironically most of us become super prayer warriors when confronted with trials or afflictions. Rather than seek the Lord (His kingdom and righteousness) – when He is near – we resort to seeking Him when we might be far from Him – we pray and fast as never when afflicted; but as soon as the pain or pressure is reduced, we forget about God. To most of us, He is God when we desperately need Him. This is a costly gamble which a true child of God should never take; for there comes a time when a stubborn sinner/wicked soul will seek the Lord in vain, even if he does so with all the tears he can muster. For the scripture reminded us of Esau's dilemma: "For you know that afterward when he wanted to inherit the blessing, he was rejected, for he found no place for repentance, though he sought it diligently with tears" (Heb. 12:17). Even worse, since there is a time for every purpose, there comes a time when there will be no time to seek the Lord. As prophet Isaiah admonished thus: "Seek the LORD while He may be found, call upon Him while He is near" (Is. 55:6). And when and how does one seek the Lord? One desirous to seek the Lord must seek Him when He is near – that is every second that the seeker has breath. And this is how to seek Him: "Let the wicked forsake his way, and the unrighteous man his thoughts: and let him return unto the LORD, and He will have mercy upon him; and to our God, for He will abundantly pardon" (Is. 55:7). But he who refuses chastisement gambles with his own life, by assuming his own risk; for he may be cut off when the Lord refuses to hear his cry. As it is written: "Then they will call on me, but I will not answer; They will seek me diligently, but they will not find me. Because they hated knowledge and did not choose the fear of the LORD, they would have none of my counsel and despised my every rebuke" (Pro. 1:28-30). Again, it is written: "He who is often rebuked and hardens his neck, will suddenly be destroyed, and that without remedy" (Prov. 29:1). Therefore, this is the understanding which establishes us – put on the whole armor of God before the enemy invades. If we do this, although the enemy may bark, he can't bite.

The enemy cannot touch us if we are in spiritual agreement with God; but if our hedge is broken through sin, we invite him and the fear that accompanies him. As the Apostle Peter wrote in his first epistle: "And who is he who will harm you if you become followers of what is good?" (1 Pet. 3:13). The obvious conditional word here is "IF" – if we become followers of God; and we have learned that God cannot have fellowship with darkness (see 1 John 1:5-7). And let there be no mistake about the truth that God is with us when we are with Him – nothing can separate us from His love except us – our iniquity separates us from Him. As it is written: "But your iniquities have separated you from your God, and your sins have hidden His face from you, so that He will not hear" (Is. 59:2). Again, "But whoever denies Me before men, him I will also deny before My Father who is in heaven" (Matt. 10:33). And again, "If we endure, we shall also reign with Him. If we deny Him, He also will deny us" (2 Tim. 2:12). Most often, we walk around with broken hedges, whereby we invite the enemy. "For My people have committed two evils: They have forsaken Me, the fountain of living waters, and hewn themselves cisterns--broken cisterns that can hold no water" (Jer. 2:13). Referring to the enslavement of God's people, the prophet, Jeremiah said: "Have you not brought this on yourself, in that you have forsaken the LORD your God When He led you in the way?" (Jer. 2:17). Although God may permit trials to confront us for His just purpose, of a severer consequence is when we lead ourselves to temptation. As it is written: "Let no one say when he is tempted, "I am tempted by God"; for God cannot be tempted by evil, nor does He Himself tempt anyone. But each one is tempted when he is drawn away by his own desires and enticed. Then, when desire has conceived, it gives birth to sin; and sin, when it is full-grown, brings forth death." (James 1:13-15).

The question some people wonder is whether God permits evil or affliction. Let it be clearly understood that God is a good and just God – He does no evil. God abhors the suffering of His children; His desire is that we get an understanding of what is required of us for our own good –

so we do not perish. As it is written: "Oh, that they had such a heart in them that they would fear Me and always keep all My commandments, that it might be well with them and with their children forever!" (Deut. 5:29). So, the only reason why God set His commandments for us – just as earthly parents set rules for their children - is for our own good. God is God, and to the extent necessary for the accomplishment of His purpose, He permits afflictions (so we call them). God created both good and evil for His purpose. For it is written: "The LORD has made all for Himself, Yes, even the wicked for the day of doom" (Prov. 16:4). As God declared boldly through prophet Isaiah "I am the LORD, and there is no other; There is no God besides Me. I will gird you, though you have not known Me, that they may know from the rising of the sun to its setting That there is none besides Me. I am the LORD, and there is no other; I form the light and create darkness, I make peace and create calamity; I, the LORD, do all these things' (Is. 45:5-7).

God uses afflictions to judge the world as well as to refine and bless His children. As the Apostle Paul correctly asked "Does not the potter have power over the clay, from the same lump to make one vessel for honor and another for dishonor? What if God, wanting to show His wrath and to make His power known, endured with much longsuffering the vessels of wrath prepared for destruction, and that He might make known the riches of His glory on the vessels of mercy, which He had prepared beforehand for glory," (Rom. 9:21-23)

It is certainly worthy of joyful acceptance that affliction or trial is a correct and effective measure of our faith, relationship with God and others. It is one thing to announce to the world that we are born again Christians, who love God above all things, but it is another to pass the relevant tests. As the simple adage says, "The taste of any food is in the eating." Until we develop a spiritual attitude towards afflictions and trials, we will always fail the test of transformation to His image, leading to the bondage of spiritual fear of the unknown. Spiritual attitude enables us to patiently desire, as we wait to learn what the Lord would use the prevailing circumstance to teach us; believing fully that He is faithful who has promised that He would not leave or forsake His own and that all things work together for good to those who love Him and endure with Him.

Out of abundance of caution, lest there be any misunderstanding, I believe it is prudent to pause here to state the obvious – affliction of any kind is never perceived or accepted by any natural person as a blessing. But suffice it to say clearly that this book is written for the consumption of the elect of God – that body of born again Christians, desirous of entering God's rest. These are given to understand the mysteries of His kingdom; they understand that while affliction may be temporary, the crown of life awaits those who do not faint and mortgage their souls but endure and overcome to the end. They understand that it is a tragedy to win the battle by scheming their ways out of difficult challenges while losing the war by offending God. These are they the world and its afflictions have been crucified unto them; they are determined to endure and overcome to the end, just like their Lord, "…, who for the joy that was set before Him endured the cross, despising the shame, and has sat down at the right hand of the throne of

God" (Heb. 12:2). Also considering the afflictions endured by some key figures in the Holy Bible, are examples for us that our God reigns forever, and evil never prevails. As we read in the book of Job, even at the point his afflictions became humanly impossible to take, yet he summoned the last breath in him and answered his friends, thus: "Hold your peace with me, and let me speak, then let come on me what may! Why do I take my flesh in my teeth, and put my life in my hands? Though He slay me, yet will I trust Him...." (Job 13:13-15). Demonstrating why he is a man after God's heart, king David expressed his understanding and gratitude to God for what He used afflictions to teach him – "It is good for me that I have been afflicted, That I may learn Your statutes" (Ps.119:71). Equally, the apostle Paul masterfully displayed his keen understanding of the temporariness of afflictions when he simply labelled them as "light" – "For our light affliction, which is but for a moment, is working for us a far more exceeding and eternal weight of glory, while we do not look at the things which are seen, but at the things which are not seen. For the things which are seen are temporary, but the things which are not seen are eternal" (2 Cor. 4:17-18). The question is – how many of us see those (things) which are not seen with our fleshy eyes? That is the heart of the matter; that is what sets one who is truly born of God apart – though he is in the world, he is not of the world; and being not of the world, the prince of the world has no place in him.

Finally, we can then appreciate apostle Paul and his companions, as they graciously set an example of spiritual attitude, who referred to their sufferings thus: "We are hard-pressed on every side, yet not crushed; we are perplexed, but

21

not in despair; persecuted, but not forsaken; struck down, but not destroyed--always carrying about in the body the dying of the Lord Jesus, that the life of Jesus also may be manifested in our body" (2 Cor. 4:8-10). Considering the above, it then brings home when the Apostle Peter admonished us not to think it strange when being afflicted, or tried, as if a strange thing is happening to us (see 1 Pet. 4:12). This is especially true, since the Lord, Himself told us that that was so, from the beginning of life the evil one had always sought a way to steal, kill and destroy the followers of what is good; afflictions will certainly come, but Christ has overcome the evil one for those who are with Him (see Ps. 37:22; John 10:10, 16:33; 1 Pet. 5:8). And having the confidence to borrow from apostle Paul's closing remark and opener in Galatians chapters four and five respectively, as my conclusion of this chapter, I concur thus: "But, as he who was born according to the flesh then persecuted him who was born according to the Spirit, even so, it is now" (Gal. 4:29). "Stand fast therefore in the liberty by which Christ has made us free, and do not be entangled again with a yoke of bondage" (Gal. 5:1).

CHAPTER FIVE

GOD WILL NOT LEAVE OR FORSAKE HIS OWN

Thus, says the Lord of hosts: "Be strong and of good courage, do not fear nor be afraid of them; for the LORD your God, He is the One who goes with you. He will not leave you nor forsake you" (Deut. 31:6). Permit me to say 'Amen' to that truth; nevertheless, that promise is subject to an "IF" factor – the fact that God is with us when we are with Him, but if we forsake or deny Him, He will also forsake and deny us. It is a reciprocal relationship, whereby we get back what we put in it (see 2 Chr. 15:2; 2 Tim. 2:11-12). The topic of "IF" Factor will be treated elaborately in the next chapter of this book.

God will always deliver the righteous from all evil: for the expectation and protection of the righteous shall not be cut short, being one, and fused spiritually together with God (see Ps, 34:17-19; John 10:27-29; 2 Pet. 2:9). It is an indisputable fact that our God, the same God who divided the sea to deliver His children from their enemies, remains the same God today and forever. None can deliver from His hands nor are His hands shortened that He cannot speedily deliver His own (see Deut. 32:39; Is. 59:1). He neither grows weary, nor does He slumber, nor faints. As the prophet Isaiah wrote: "Have you not known? Have you not heard? The everlasting God, the LORD, The Creator of the ends of the earth, neither faints nor is weary. His understanding is unsearchable" (Is. 40:28). Again, as said by the Lord in the book of Isaiah "Why, when I came, was there no man? Why, when I called, was there none to answer? Is My hand shortened at all that it cannot redeem? Or have I no power to deliver? Indeed, with My rebuke I dry up the sea, I make the rivers a wilderness......" (Is. 50:2).

Our God is undoubtedly the most dependable, reliable, faithful, trustworthy, and predictable – for He does not change. Unlike man, God's one plus one will always remain two. He is the only One who swears by His word – He does whatever He says, and He remains faithful even when we become unfaithful (see Is. 55:8-11, Mal. 3:6; Matt. 24:35; James 1:17). I can testify with confident assurance that if I live a life always pleasing to Him (always doing His will in implicit obedience), God will surely reciprocate with His loving kindness and mercy towards me, including but not limited to, His divine hedge, even without praying. As it is written: "Look to Me and be saved, all you ends of the earth! For I am God, and there is no other. I have sworn by Myself; The word has gone out of My mouth in righteousness, and shall not return, that to Me every knee [including the devil's knee] shall bow, every tongue shall take an oath" (Is. 45:22-23). Again, God and His word are inseparably one; if God's word fails, God has failed. And we know and believe that it is impossible for God to change or fail, being the Ancient of Days. If there be any consolation, it is in this – we can boast and testify truthfully of God's awesome and righteous deliverance of His people. As it is written: "But without faith, it is impossible to please Him, for he who comes to God must believe that He is and that He is a rewarder of those who diligently seek Him" (Heb. 11:6).

Our God is zealously jealous for His true children; for with a mighty hand, He delivered and still delivers the children of Israel from their enemies. He delivered David from the hands of King Saul who sought after his life. He delivered Job and restored Job from the hand of Satan; He delivered Daniel who later testified of God's awesome deliverance, thus: "My God sent His angel and shut the lions' mouths, so that they have not hurt me, because I was found innocent before Him; and also, O king, I have done no wrong before you" (Dan. 6:22).

The Book of Daniel further recorded an epic demonstration of absolute faith and trust in God by Shadrach, Meshach, and Abed-Nego, and God's marvelous reciprocal deliverance of them from King Nebuchadnezzar's burning furnace (see Dan. 3:14-30). King Nebuchadnezzar was so marveled at God's deliverance of these three just men of God, that he acknowledged thus: "Nebuchadnezzar spoke, saying, "Blessed be the God of Shadrach, Meshach, and Abed-Nego, who sent His Angel and delivered His servants who trusted in Him, and they have frustrated the king's word, and yielded their bodies, that they should not serve nor worship any god except their own God" (Dan. 3:28)! It is noteworthy that the uniqueness of these true children/servants of God who were beneficiaries of His mighty deliverances was that they were all perfect in unreserved submission to God before the enemy unleashed his attack. As it is written in the epistle of James: "Therefore submit to God [submit first to God]. Resist the devil, and he will flee from you" (James 4:7). In other words, put on the whole armor of God first, that is, being one with God through implicit obedience, and He will not leave or forsake you; rather, your battle becomes His battle, and He will surely deliver you and give you victory over the enemy (see Eph. 6:10-18).

The three instances of divine deliverance mentioned above are demonstrative of the fact that God is always able, and does deliver His saints from forces of darkness. We must carefully note the more ministering revelation relative to these deliverances, therefore, we should pause to examine carefully the reason Daniel cited for God's deliverance. He said that he (Daniel) lived a life that God found to be innocent in His eyes even before he (Daniel) was thrown into the lion's den. Daniel's three brethren, Shadrach, Meshach, and Abed-Nego exhibited absolute faith and trust in, and reverence for His name, so much so that they were ready to be incinerated in the fiery burning furnace, if it was God's will. They maintained and encouraged themselves in their God, by doing all things to His glory, rather than bow to an idol in fear of the king (a man who could only destroy the flesh and couldn't save himself). Their response at that breaking point is so chilling and powerful that it puts most of us (our faith in God) to shame. As it is written: "If that is the case, our God whom we serve is able to deliver us from the burning fiery furnace, and He will deliver us from your hand, O king. But if not, let it be known to you, O king, that we do not serve your gods, nor will we worship the gold image which you have set up" (Dan. 3:17-18). In other words, these uncompromisingly faithful men believed absolutely that their God was not only able to, and would deliver them; but in the event, that He chose not to deliver them, He was still their God. That is for good or for bad, He remains our God, able to do whatever glorifies His Holy name. The psalmist, King David, was always full of praises of God for delivering Him from the hands of His enemies.

The new Testament is also clustered with God's deliverances of His saints from the jaws of their enemies: from apostle Peter's release from prison to innumerable deliverances of apostle Paul from enemies within and without, including principalities of all kinds (see Acts 12:1-11, 28:1-6).

Recounting his sufferings and God's faithful deliverances, apostle Paul wrote thus: "Are they ministers of Christ? --I speak as a fool--I am more: in labors more abundant, in stripes above measure, in prisons more frequently, in deaths often. From the Jews five times I received forty stripes minus one. Three times I was beaten with rods; once I was stoned; three times I was shipwrecked; a night and a day I have been in the deep; in journeys often, in perils of waters, in perils of robbers, in perils of my own countrymen, in perils of the Gentiles, in perils in the city, in perils in the wilderness, in perils in the sea, in perils among false brethren...." (2 Cor. 11:23-26…33). The apostle Paul suffered so many afflictions that prompted him to declare: "For we do not want you to be ignorant, brethren, of our trouble which came to us in Asia: that we were burdened beyond measure, above strength, so that we despaired even of life" (2 Cor. 1:8). Yet, despite all the afflictions and attacks by the enemy and his agents, he referred to them as "…light affliction, which is but for a moment, is working for us a far more exceeding and eternal weight of glory," (2 Cor. 4:17). In other words, if we learn to set our minds firmly on the ultimate prize (eternal glory), and accept the fact that affliction is for a moment, and no one can deliver or take from God's hands, victory will always be ours at the end of it all. It was on the basis of this firm belief and consolation that informed apostle Paul's declaration in his second epistle to Timothy: "…persecutions, afflictions, which happened to me at Antioch, at Iconium, at Lystra--what persecutions I endured. And out of them all the Lord delivered me" (2 Tim. 3:11).

The apostle peter also assured us that God will always deliver His own from attacks and temptations: "…then the Lord knows how to deliver the godly out of temptations and to reserve the unjust under punishment for the day of judgment" (2 Pet. 2:9).

As the Lord assured in the gospel according to John: "These things, I have spoken to you, that in Me you may have peace. In the world you will have tribulation; but be of good cheer, I have overcome the world" (John 16:33). The apostles, who were pillars of the body of Christ, suffered many spiritual and physical attacks, as all who are truly in Christ must suffer: but of more importance is the fact that they prevailed until God's appointed time, because they were one, in spiritual agreement with God, having mortified all fleshly lusts, distractions, and affections of this world.

Therefore, we must be confidently grateful and assured that God would not fail to deliver His true children from all attacks of the devil; and if He restrains His hand, He does so to fulfill His purpose, for our good and His glory (see Rom. 9:11-23). It is worthy of acceptance that, spiritually speaking, it is of no consequence what we suffer or endure, but rather what we become thus thereof. Affliction is the most refining tool in the hands of God. When afflictions, torments, and attacks come, for they must surely come, we must remain prayerfully patient, so that we can learn what God wants to accomplish in our lives with them. Afflictions get us to consider and mend our ways, as well as test our resolve, faith, and love for God. The apostle Paul had to learn this crucial lesson, as he intimates us on how he besought God thrice to remove Satan's thorn in his flesh, and God, while refusing to oblige him, however, assured him that His grace and strength were sufficient for him (see 2 Cor.12:7-9). Now, whatever 'this thing' (the thorn in Paul's flesh) was is of no spiritual consequence or significance to us. What is significant was what Paul learned and became because of his experience. The experience so humbled Paul that he declared: "…. Therefore, most gladly I will rather boast in my infirmities, that the power of Christ may rest upon me. Therefore, I take pleasure in infirmities, in reproaches, in needs, in persecutions, in distresses, for Christ's sake. For when I am weak, then I am strong [in the Lord]" (2 Cor. 12:9-10). No wonder, apostle Paul boasted confidently that he could do all things through Christ which strengthened him (see Phil. 4:13).

I must add in conclusion, as confidently as we are that God is a faithful covenant keeper and deliverer of those who are His, the critical question is – who are His? Those who are God's are those born of and led by His Spirit; they are those spiritually fused together in agreement with Him through implicit obedience to His commandments – they believe and abide in Him, and His words abide in them – being one and always doing His will (see John 3:5-6, 8:31, 14:15, 15:7, 14; 1 John 3:24). For we know Him who said: "I love those who love Me…." (Prov. 8:17); "And He who sent Me is with Me. The Father has not left Me alone, for I always do those things that please Him" (John 8:29). In other words, our

Lord said that the Father would have left Him (Christ) if He did not please Him (Father) always. And if that was the case with the only begotten Son of God, why do we think God will remain with us when we forsake or deny Him?

And with these encouraging and uplifting words of consolation and caution, let us go to the next chapter to examine the "IF" factor of God.

CHAPTER SIX

THE IF FACTOR

Oh, what a merciful, gracious, and long-suffering God we have; His steadfast love never ceases, His mercies never come to an end, they are new all the time - indeed great is His faithfulness (see Lam. 3:22-23). This is certainly true of our awesome, trustworthy and dependable God; for even when we are ungratefully unfaithful, He remains faithful and unchangeable (see 2 Tim. 2:12-13). Our God is also a consuming fire; He is fearful in praises and terrible in punishment. He will never change for anyone or nation. He remains the same. Responding to Moses's intercession for his disobedient and rebellious brethren, the LORD said: "I have pardoned, according to your word; but truly, as I live, all the earth shall be filled with the glory of the LORD-- because all these men who have seen My glory and the signs which I did in Egypt and in the wilderness, and have put Me to the test now these ten times, and have not heeded My voice, they certainly shall not see the land of which I swore to their fathers, nor shall any of those who rejected Me see it. But My servant Caleb, because he has a different spirit in him and has followed Me fully, I will bring into the land where he went, and his descendants shall inherit it" (Num. 14:20-24).

Although all good things and blessings come from Him, there is neither any variation in nor partiality with Him (see James 1:17; 1 Pet. 1:17). These verses are loaded with two serious admonishments. The apostle Peter wanted to seriously remind us that (a) there is no partiality whatsoever with God, (b) we should remain ever vigilantly and soberly careful to always abide in Him. The apostle Peter was echoing God's consistent warning from the book of Genesis to the book of Revelation, that we should never take Him for granted, but always observe to do His will, lest we be consumed. As the Psalmist also wrote: "Serve the LORD with fear and rejoice with trembling" (Ps. 2:11). The apostle Paul also sounded the same warning: "Therefore, my beloved, as you have always obeyed, not as in my presence only, but now much more in my absence, work out your own salvation with fear and trembling" (Phil. 2:12). On the same note, the Lord cautioned His jubilant disciples who came back in celebration mode because the demons were subject to them in His name, thus: "Nevertheless do not rejoice in this, that the spirits are subject to you, but rather rejoice because your names are written in heaven" (Luke 10:20).

Therefore, caveat emptor – let the buyer beware, and make no mistake about it, whoever ignores the obvious fact that our God, the Ancient of Days is a God of "IF," does assume his own risk of death. "IF" is the cornerstone of all God's promises and covenants: it is the dominant, indispensable and inexpungible word that makes God's promises or covenants conditional. Every promise or covenant of God contains the "IF" word, a condition precedent to God's performance. Sadly, it is this indispensable word of God that the enemy has succeeded in getting "feel good," prosperity, motivational gospel preachers, and most churches to frown at and conveniently eliminate from their vocabulary. These enemies of the cross present unwholesome false gospel and doctrine that "once saved, always saved," regardless of what we do on this earth thereafter. They tell their captive audiences to go ahead and live it all out, and be all they can be on this earth because Christ has forgiven all our past, present, and future sins; therefore, there remains no more need of repentance or obedience. What a blatant false doctrine. For if that doctrine of false sense of security is true, we are already in heaven, because Christ has paid it all, and gave us the license to reproach His Father, whom He is one with. For why would one work out his own salvation with fear and trembling if he is so sure that from the day he accepted Christ as Lord, his salvation was guaranteed to the end, regardless of what he does thereafter. Why then do the first become last? (see Matt. 19:30). Why would a barren branch that is already in Christ be taken away; and why would the unprofitable servant and those who bear bad fruits be cut down and cast into hell fire? As it is written: "But he who endures to the end will be saved" (Matt. 10:22, 24:13). "I am the true vine, and My Father is the vinedresser. Every branch in Me that does not bear fruit He takes away; and every branch that bears fruit He prunes, that it may bear more fruit" (John 15:1-2). "Every tree that does not bear good fruit is cut down and thrown into the fire" (Matt. 7:19). "So take the talent from him [the unprofitable servant], and give it to him who has ten talents. 'For to everyone who has, more will be given, and he will have abundance; but from him who does not have, even what he has will be taken away. And cast the unprofitable servant [mind you, he was already a servant] into the outer darkness. There will be weeping and gnashing of teeth" (Matt. 25:28-30).

Have we not heard that many would be called, but few would be chosen? Were not all Israelites saved from Egyptian bondage, but how many entered the promised land? (see 1 Cor. 10:1-12; Jude 1:5). Have we not read that the five foolish virgins were not allowed to enter His rest, despite the fact they got to the end [not according to His prescribed rule, though they were virgins]? It is also written for our own admonishment, that whoever looks back while in this eternal race will be disqualified without mercy (see Luke 9: 62; Heb. 10:36-38). The scripture warns us that if a righteous man relies on his righteousness, and commits iniquity and dies in it, all his past righteousness shall not be remembered (see Ezek. 18:24, 33:12-13). Does it even come to our comprehension that if God did not spare His servant Moses, the one who saw His back, that He might not spare us too, if we continue in disobedience? (see Deut. 3:23-29). The apostle Paul stated that he obtained mercy from God because the evil deeds he did were done in ignorance (see 1 Tim. 1:13). But after we have known the truth, we become bound by it (sin); thereby making all our present sins presumptuous in nature, and a reproach to God. "But the person who does anything presumptuously, whether he is native-born or a stranger, that one brings reproach on the LORD, and he shall be cut off from among his people. Because he has despised the word of the LORD and has broken His commandment, that person shall be completely cut off; his guilt shall be upon him" (Num. 15:30-31). One who sins presumptuously has decided to insult the Spirit of grace, hence the writer of Hebrews says that there remains no more sacrifice for such sin (see Heb. 6:3-6, 10:26-29). We are all privy of the Lord's saying in the Book of Revelation, that He sits on His Father's throne because He overcame to the end; and all who want to be with Him must overcome by keeping His word to the end. "And he who overcomes, and keeps My works until the end, to him I will give power over the nations--" (Rev. 2:26). Again, "To him who overcomes I will grant to sit with Me on My throne, as I also overcame and sat down with My Father on His throne" (Rev. 3:21) It will not be an over-emphasis to remind us that our Lord says that he who keeps His works until the end, is the one who has overcome (see Rev. 2:26). He who has an ear in his heart, let him hear what the Lord says to His elect.

The other false doctrine relative to this chapter is the notion that all the blessings of Abraham are ours, without the sufferings or obedience of Abraham. The "feel good, and prosperity" preachers deceive their captive congregations in believing that God's covenant is a covenant of free for all blessings and prosperity, and all you need do to grab them is to "declare and claim" them. They say that God is in the business of blessing and healing His children. But I know that God truly blesses and heals His children, and I also know that His true business is eternal salvation of souls, so that none will perish. But can one declare or claim what he does not have or own? For us to inherit God's blessings, we must abide by the law of "IF" - by first performing or satisfying or fulfilling the condition precedent to the release of His blessings.

Our relationship with God is of a dependence nature. A covenant is a form of agreement, and it is required of every agreement to embody certain considerations and performances, provisions, to be met or executed by parties who have a meeting of the mind. Hence, it is written: "Can two walk together, unless they are agreed?" (Amos 3:3). The word "IF" (conditional) implies a condition precedent or an element of consideration or a performance dependent on the prior performance or act of some form, and until such condition is performed, the other party is not under obligation to perform. Let me state boldly, that God's most important business, desire, or blessing is eternal life – eternity with Him – that which is everlasting and imperishable. Earthly blessings to his children are the least of God's concern, for He owns heaven and earth, and although He can dish out earthly blessings to His children as

He wishes, He considers those things secondary and insignificant. Hence, He has urged us to lay hold of eternal life first, and all other needs shall be added to us (see Matt. 6:33). Sadly, and abominably, most churches have been turned into buying and selling zones, with different forms of craftily designed money exchange formulae to satisfy covetous appetite. In just about all "feel good," and prosperity churches, the only resemblance to Christ is when the preachers mention His name in attempts to get their congregations to concur with "AMEN." Usually, the weekly or bi-weekly re-occurring gospel message is a carefully sugar coated litany or grocery lists of all the promised blessings of God. These preachers engage their captive audiences to repetitively recite or chant God's promised mercies, favors, goodness, earthly blessings and miracles, while leaving out or eliminating entirely portions that deal with what God requires of His children to do first before His blessings would overtake them.

I have had many privileges of ministering to congregations, where their pastors or bishops craftily dosed out a litany of these endless blessings and promises, citing scriptures in part – and you guess which parts – the sweetened parts, while the conditions parts which require individual duty or responsibility were never mentioned. I recall now, as if it were yesterday, one notable incident where the congregation was asked to read projected verses of chapter twenty-six of the third book of Moses, called Leviticus. Surprisingly, the reading began from verse four, reading all the wonderful blessings of God, and concluded with verse thirteen. When eventually I got up to minister to the congregation, I firmly asked the presiding bishop why he decided to leave out verse three, which verses four through thirteen are dependent on: "If you walk in My statutes and keep My commandments, and perform them," (Lev. 26:3); and verse fourteen down, which spell out all the curses which would befall the people if they rebelled and disobeyed. To my uttermost shock, the bishop told me that the verses I referred to "are not our portion." Needless to state that after painfully telling all that God had appointed to hear, that God is a God of "IF" and with Him, "it is all or nothing," the merciful God, who knows His own, touched and converted many souls to Himself.

My experience with another "feel good," and prosperity church was similar but with a different response. The presiding pastor had his congregation on cloud nine, shouting and screaming for joy when they concluded their partial reading of the fifth book of Moses called Deuteronomy, chapter twenty-eight, where even part of verse one through verse thirteen was read. They left out the part in verse one which reads: "Now it shall come to pass, if you diligently obey the voice of the LORD your God, to observe carefully all His commandments which I command you today..." (Deut. 28:1), but read only the sweet part, "that the LORD your God will set you high above all nations of the earth." (Deuteronomy 28:13). Finally, they repeated verse thirteen over and over, and neither read it in full nor ever uttered the word "IF" that is embedded in the verse. Rather, they heralded and celebrated their inheritance of being made "the head and not the tail"; "above only, not beneath." "Now it shall come to pass, if you diligently obey the voice of the LORD your God, to observe carefully all His commandments which I command you today, that the LORD your God will set you high above all nations of the earth" (Deut. 28:1) "But it shall come to pass, if you do not obey the voice of the Lord your God, to observe carefully all His commandments and His statutes which I command you today, that all these curses will come upon you and overtake you" (Deut. 28:15). Again, like the first church above, this later church conveniently suppressed the rest of the chapter, verse fourteen through verse sixty-eight, which carefully enumerated various curses which would befall the rebellious and disobedient.

These houses of "feel good," and prosperity gospel are mere houses of lies and covetousness. It is accepted fact that no lie can be of the truth: and there is nothing against the truth but the truth (see 2 Cor. 13:8; 1 John 2:21). Ninety-nine percent (99%) truth is still a lie; so also, half bread is no bread to God, just as partial transformation is zero transformation. As the Lord commands, "But let your 'Yes' be 'Yes,' and your 'No,' 'No.' For whatever is more than these is from the evil one" (Matt. 5:37). Therefore, whoever preaches, practices or encourages unwholesome doctrine contrary to the undiluted and uncompromising gospel/word of Christ, is a liar; and being a liar, he is of the devil, since the devil is the father of liars (see Matt. 24:23-26; John 8:44; Col. 2:8; 1 Tim. 6:3-5; 2 Tim. 3:1-5; 2 John 1:9-11).

UNAVOIDABLE, UNIDENTICAL, BUT INSEPARABLE TWINS

There are two unavoidable, inseparable, unidentical twins - blessing and curse. They both constitute an inseparable coin of two different sides. Where there is a blessing, a curse is associated with it. Even with God, there is no free lunch. As the saying goes, where there is no pain, there is no gain. It is usually a blessing or a curse, 'IF'; they go hand in hand. In the beginning, Adam and Eve were entitled to all the goodness and blessings of God, if they diligently continued as commanded, not to eat of the fruit of the tree of the knowledge of good and evil (see Gen. 3:16-17). We can choose to obey and be showered with His blessings, or receive His wrath because of disobedience. As it is written: "If you are willing and obedient, you shall eat the good of the land; But if you refuse and rebel, you shall be devoured by the sword"; For the mouth of the LORD has spoken" (Is. 1:19-20). God's blessings will overflow us if we keep His commandments; but if we choose to disobey, His curses will also overtake us. It is this simple reality that most "feel good" and prosperity preachers want to hide from their itching ear audience. Therefore, they preach what they think or know people want to hear, so that in return, they get what they want from them. Whoever preaches to please people, rather than to please God, is a servant of men, not of God. And it is usually the case that servants of men are servants to their belly and pocket. We must choose whom we would serve –

for we cannot serve two masters; neither is it permissible to run around professing we are servants of God, while indeed we serve money. As Moses laid it straight to the children of Israel: "Behold, I set before you today a blessing and a curse: the blessing, if you obey the commandments of the LORD your God which I command you today; and the curse, if you do not obey the commandments of the LORD your God, but turn aside from the way which I command you today, to go after other gods which you have not known" (Deut. 11:26-28).. Even in our relationship with Him, we are His disciples and friends if we keep His commandments (see John 8:31, 15:14); if we diligently keep His commandments, without turning to the right or to the left, our God will bless us and our children. He will also heal us and our land (see Deut. 5:29, 10:12-13; 2 Chr. 7:14); He will forgive us if we forgive others, but if we refuse to forgive all people, He will in turn not forgive us, and may even retract His prior forgiveness (see Matt. 6:14-15, 18:33-35).

I appeal to all those who are victims of this unwholesome gospel to flee from these preachers and churches, lest they be consumed with them. Therefore, as it is written: "If anyone teaches otherwise and does not consent to wholesome words, even the words of our Lord Jesus Christ, and to the doctrine which accords with godliness, he is proud, knowing nothing, but is obsessed with disputes and arguments over words, from which come envy, strife, reviling, evil suspicions, useless wranglings of men of corrupt minds and destitute of the truth, who suppose that godliness is a means of gain. From such withdraw yourself"

(1 Tim. 6:3-5). "But know this, that in the last days, perilous times will come: For men will be lovers of themselves, lovers of money, boasters, proud, blasphemers, disobedient to parents, unthankful, unholy, unloving, unforgiving, slanderers, without self-control, brutal, despisers of good, traitors, headstrong, haughty, lovers of pleasure rather than lovers of God, having a form of godliness but denying its power. And from such people turn away!" (2 Tim. 3:1-5).

CHAPTER SEVEN

ORIGIN OF SPIRITUAL FEAR OF THE UNKNOWN

We have noted that if Satan ever deserves any credit at all, it is that he is relentlessly resilient and persistent in the pursuit of his destructive course and tendencies; and that no one is immune from his attacks. Although he trembles at the name of God, nevertheless, that does not preclude him from trying, in the hope that he might succeed. Satan is a master of the adage which states. "If you fail, try, try and try again." For his self-assigned mission, as the scripture says, is to ceaselessly wander the earth seeking whom (a prey) to devour (see Job 1:7; 1 Pet. 5:8). Now consider the share audacity Satan had in tempting our Lord Jesus Christ, knowing fully He (Christ) was the Son of God. Therefore, to unmask this monstrous bondage to spiritual fear of the unknown, it is of necessity, I suppose, to treat its origin as the heart of the matter.

It is a known and prudent fact that to successfully cure a disease, one must understand its source or origin. The chance of winning a battle against an unknown or imaginary enemy is close to zero. It is he who understands a terrain that leads its trails. So, what is the origin or source of this devastating evil called spiritual fear? It is therefore very prudent and urgent for us to endeavor to obtain a clear and conclusive understanding of the origin of spiritual fear – this evil phenomenon, which for long has robbed people and nations of the developing world, especially Africa, of peace, joy, progress and development. The scripture says that people perish for lack of knowledge (see Hos. 4:6). Nevertheless, the scripture further reminds us that even wisdom and knowledge will fail without understanding. As it is written "Wisdom is the principal thing; therefore, get wisdom. And in all your getting, get understanding" (Prov. 4:7). Again, it is written: "Through wisdom, a house is built, and by understanding it is established" (Prov. 24:3). Understanding then is the realization of wisdom, knowledge, and discretion. Hence the scripture says that wisdom finds house in the heart of one who has understanding (see Prov. 14:33). The Book of Job gives a more practical and vivid meaning of the distinction between wisdom and understanding, to wit: while the fear of God is wisdom, to depart from evil is understanding that establishes (see Job 28:28). Putting it another way, to go to church and profess to know God is mere wisdom, but to obey all He has commanded to do is understanding. For it is not what we say, but we are known by what we do.

SPIRITUAL FEAR IS NOT HEREDITARY

Generally, it is most naturally and reasonably expected of anyone, regardless of race, color or geographical location to desperately deploy lifesaving schemes to preserve life when faced with a threat or perceived threat. It is, I believe, a fair and conclusive statement that there is a reasonable measure of common (natural) fear trait in humans, irrespective of their race, environment and upbringing. A typical example is a common fear of falling from a considerable height, in both babies and adults. However, it is equally true that superficial, imaginary and spiritual fear of the unknown is unreasonable. Sadly, and unfortunately, spiritual fear – this debilitating enslavement of the mind is more prevalent, if not somehow an exclusive problem of some developing nations, particularly in Africa. I suppose it will amount to a heresy, devoid of any substantive evidence or proof, to suggest, as some in certain quarters ought to do, that spiritual fear is either hereditary or due to a generational curse. Can it be said that spiritual fear of the unknown is hereditary? God forbid!

We believe the scripture that God created all people in His image and likeness, irrespective of their ethnicity and different geographical and environmental locations. As it is written: "So God created man in His own image; in the image of God He created him; male and female He created them" (Gen. 1:27). One wonders aloud why spiritual fear of the unknown – this monstrous destroyer of the mind, appears to be a debilitating foe of people, particularly in Sub-Saharan Africa. It is noteworthy that children of African descent born in Europe and United States of America, for example, are fortunately not saddled with this evil, called spiritual fear of the unknown. These children are our own bone of bones and flesh of flesh. They were born free and innocent children as those of their mates in Africa, yet no sooner these children born and reared in certain parts of Africa reach the age of five, if not younger, depending on tribal, cultural and traditional practices and belief, they become unwittingly initiated into the bondage of spiritual fear, while their counterparts in Europe and United States retain their sound minds (relative to spiritual fear of the unknown). The difference is our children born and reared in these developed nations are never drilled and imbibed in spiritual fear. Rather if and whenever they experience setbacks or nightmares, they simply shrug them off as nightmares or failure on their own part. If they fail, they pick themselves right up and try again until they succeed. They believe that they are responsible for their success or failure; therefore, they do not resign and succumb to imaginary and insurmountable spiritual opposition, which is remotely sent by imaginary spirits or enemies (most of who are usually relatives, and other "giants" opposed to their advancement and progress) to "tie" their fortunes. All these they do while still retaining their sound minds. The most interesting part is that the parents of these children were born and reared in Africa. So, what is amiss? For the scripture tells us that good fruits are produced by good trees, while bad trees bear only bad fruits (see Matt 7:17-18). It, therefore, leads one to an obvious conclusion that something is fundamentally wrong when children born to African parents who are in bondage to spiritual fear, but living in Europe or the United States, are free from such bondage, but their counterparts in these developing nations are saddled with the bondage of spiritual fear.

As for the children born and reared in these developing nations infested with spiritual fear of the unknown, they strongly and detrimentally hold on to the belief that nothing happens without an underlying spiritual or human (usually their enemies) interference. They strongly and defiantly believe that there is no unpleasant incident unassociated with 'remote' spiritual course. For example, no one suffers a terminal illness without some remote spiritual or human cause; neither does one die of a natural cause, nor does a student fail a course without the remote undoing of an uncle or another relation; nor does a business fail absent of an enemy who has either succeeded in "tying" the business owners' fortune, or a sign of an urgent need to appease one spirit or the other (most notably, spirits of late fathers or grandfathers). Rather than conduct autopsy on the dead, they exhaustively expend their time and meager resources trying to figure out which of their wicked enemies remotely caused the demise of their relation or invoked a bad spirit to kill the deceased.

The problem of these enslaved children usually begins from early childhood, when their parents would drill, instill and imbibe spiritual fear of the unknown into their heads and psyche. These parents and others in these societies would pass on (non-genetically) spiritual fear to their innocent, but unfortunate children, one generation to the next. The process of passing on this evil to children is usually by verbal and ritualistic instructions, stories, sacrifices, initiations and other local practices. We therefore boldly conclude that spiritual fear of the unknown is neither hereditary nor is it because of generational curse; rather, it is learned, taught, induced, reinforced and passed from one generation to another generation by parents, relatives, idol priests and more so now than ever before, agents of darkness and covetousness, parading themselves as ministers and servants of Christ. It is abominable to state the obvious, that many leaders of the very institution (church) whose commission is to set the captive free, have conveniently made themselves agents of bondage for their pecuniary gain. With spiritual fear, the level of idolatry and other forms of cultural and traditional initiation in a society, tribe or region, determines the level of bondage to spiritual fear and ignorance

The Rooster Illustration – Believing in the Devil

Some years past, on my way to a church revival conference, the Lord instructed me to tell the congregation to raise for Him "a generation of gods, free from bondage of the mind." Further, the Lord told me that most Christians in Africa believe in the devil and are like the big rooster that runs away terrified at the slightest approach, or mere imagination of appearance or presence of a kite in the air. And when I shared these revelations with the congregation, I was not surprised there was indignation before they finally understood. You see, whoever we believe in his works and such belief influences us tremendously, especially when such works cause us to fear and dismay in us, spiritually, we believe in the person. Therefore, when we say that we do not believe in the devil, but we believe in his works – so much that such belief influences and controls our mind considerably, in truth, we believe in him, for the devil and his works are the same. When the apostle Philip asked the Lord to show them the Father, the Lord answered among other things: "Believe Me that I am in the Father and the Father in Me, or else believe Me for the sake of the works themselves" (John 14:11).

In rural villages, the rooster is both the king of birds, as well as an alarm clock, or even the village crier. Without fail, or rather the first sound in the morning, the rooster (cock) exercises its natural duty as it asserts its supremacy with its flapping wings and loud crows. But no sooner a small kite appears or is imagined to appear above, the big rooster runs for dear life, shamelessly gripped with paralyzing fear of death. You see, although the poor rooster has grown beyond the ability of a kite to carry it away, it remains still in bondage, and as such it will never be free, despite its noisy crows. Like our rooster which acquired and learned its fear of kite from mama hen, our spiritual fear of the unknown is learned and acquired; and if the scales of spiritual fear are not removed from our mind, we will never know the truth that sets us free.

CHAPTER EIGHT

NO GENERATIONAL CURSE

Let me affirm boldly, confidently and unequivocally, that contrary to infamous teachings and practices of anti-Christ ministers, ministries, and churches of bondage and houses of deliverance, liberation, deception and manipulation, in Christ Jesus – there is no generational curse.

Generational curse, the two words which have been deployed by agents of the devil parading themselves in most developing nations, especially Africa, as servants of God to reinforce and perpetuate spiritual fear, in their abominable and covetous deception, control mechanism, manipulation, and lies. Sadly, these agents of darkness have perfected their craftiness by fashioning generational curse as the most potent weapon in their arsenal of manipulation, deception, and abuse of their vulnerable victims, who unfortunately number in millions.

Generational curse is undoubtedly the preferred weapon of false prophets and prophetess, also running in millions all over Africa and some other developing nations. Their aim is to tap on and reinforce their doctrine for the effective enslavement of any unfortunate soul who ventures into their trap.

While the only purpose of a true servant of God is to turn people away from their evil ways to God, by teaching them the undiluted word of God, the knowledge (implicit obedience) of which sets the captive free from bondage, instead, these wicked agents have turned the institution (church) into a place of corruption and worthless rituals and merchandising (see Is. 61:1-3; Jer. 6:13-16; 7:9-11; 23:21-22).

Let us take a closer and careful look at chapter sixty-one, verse one through three of the Book of Isaiah (Is. 61:1-3) which scriptures were cited by our Lord Jesus Christ in the fourth chapter, verses eighteen and nineteen of the gospel according to Luke (Lk 4:18-19). The commission the Lord has given to His true servants is to preach (live and preach) the truth to the poor, not mislead them; to heal the sick, not take advantage of, abuse, or kill them; to proclaim liberty, not to enslave the captives; to set the bound free, not to erect an imaginary and invisible prison wall against them; to comfort and console all who mourn, not inflict irreparable and irreversible damage to them; to be the light and example of righteousness and holiness for people to behold and glorify the name of God, not blaspheme and put Him to an open shame; and did I mention to feed the flock not eat them? This I say and affirm truthfully that even assuming for argument only, that there is a generational curse, there is no number of worthless rituals that can set a person or a family or village or a people free, except the knowledge of the truth in Christ (living and being the truth). As it is written "And you shall know the truth and the truth shall make you free" (John 8:32). And whosoever that is made free by the knowledge of the truth (living the word/truth) which is in Christ is free indeed for all purposes. (see John 8:36). "And this is eternal life, that they may know You, the only true God and Jesus Christ whom You have sent" (John 17:3).

To know the truth/God (not know of Him) is to love Him, and to know Him is to implicitly obey all He has commanded us to observe to do. Our Lord was very emphatic about this with the multitude that came to hear Him. "Yet you have not known Him, but I know Him: and if I say I do not know Him, I shall be a liar like you: but I do know Him and keep His word" (John 8:55). Again, as the Apostle John writes in his first epistle, "Now by this, we know that we know Him if we keep His commandments. He who says I know Him and does not keep His commandments is a liar, and the truth is not him" (1 John 2:3-4).

As stated inter alia, the only purpose of God's servant is to teach people the truth, the knowledge of which sets them free from bondage (see Matt 28:19-20). So, whoever puts another in bondage of fear of the unknown is not of God. As it is written in the second epistle of the apostle Peter, "But there were also false prophets among the people, even as there will be false teachers among you, who will secretly bring in destructive heresies, even denying the Lord who bought them, and bring upon themselves swift destruction. And many will follow their destructive ways, because of whom the way of truth will be blasphemed. By covetousness they will exploit you with deceptive words; for a long time their judgment has not been idle, and their destruction does not slumber" (2 Pet 2:1-3).

GOD NEVER ORDAINED OR COMMANDED GENERATIONAL CURSE

It is time to pause with open and unreserved mind and submission to the infallible authority of the scriptures, since arguably we accept that "All Scripture is given by inspiration of God, and is profitable for doctrine, for reproof, for correction, for instruction in righteousness, that the man of God may be complete, thoroughly equipped for every good work" (2 Tim 3:16-17). For two years, the blunt teaching of this liberating truth at various conferences has sent shock waves on most ministers of the word, while it brought divine liberty to their captive audiences.

As stated before, permit me to boldly state again, without any shadow of doubt or any risk of contradiction whatsoever that as a general rule/commandment, our just God never intended, neither ordained, commanded, nor approved the unjust imputation of any one's righteousness or unrighteousness to another. Every soul shall be judged and rewarded in strict accordance with the deeds he/she alone has done, not the deeds of another. The iniquities of a person shall not be visited on another innocent soul. Let me also state that as an exception, God, who does whatever pleases Him may visit the sins of a father on his family. The issue here is the imputation of righteousness, or unrighteousness, curse or blessing on a person, based on the actions of another person. No one gains righteousness or eternal life based on their father's or mother's righteousness; neither does God consider it just that anyone be condemned by the unrighteousness or evil deeds of their parents. Again, let it be known that there is no established commandment of God for generational curse. As a general principle, God does not punish the innocent soul, but a soul that deliberately sins, that soul shall die. The greatest desire of God is that no soul should perish. Some ministers who reinforce generational curse do so either due to lack of spiritual understanding of the scriptures and mysteries of God's kingdom, while most of them use it for control, advantage and pecuniary gain – they employ it to promote fear, bondage, which in turn perpetuates their demonic and covetous enterprise.

Our God is a just, holy, righteous God; He never desires the loss of souls because of the deeds of another. He has explicitly and expressly stated, from the beginning to the end – from the Book of Genesis to Revelation of Jesus Christ, that generational curse is contrary to His commandments. Therefore, the reinforcement, or preaching, or teaching of generational curse is contrary to the commandments of God and the gospel of Jesus Christ. Those who are ministers and proponents of generational curse usually and strongly rely on the provisions of Exodus, chapter twenty, verses four and five (Ex. 20:4-5). We note in these verses that God's first recorded commandment is against idol worship of any kind; and in expressing an alter abhorrence of idolatry worship, He said among other things; "You shall not make for yourself a carved image – any likeness of anything that is in heaven above, or that is in the earth beneath, or that is in the water under the earth; You shall not bow down to them nor serve them. For I, the Lord your God am a jealous God visiting the iniquity of the fathers upon the children to the third and fourth generations of those who hate Me, (Ex. 20:4-5). Unfortunately, the re-enforcers of generational curse stop here, not having understanding that the preceding sentence is incomplete without verse six, which follows the punctuation icon 'coma,' which reads as follows: "but showing mercy to thousand to those who love Me and keep My commandments" (Ex. 20:6). In other words, anyone who worships idol hates God; and whoever hates God is under a curse. In simplest words, if one who is cursed because he hates God begets children who follow their father's wicked ways, they are cursed, not because of what their father does, but rather because of what they do against God. However, to the extent any of those children rejects and abhors his father's iniquity and turns to love God by implicitly obeying His commandments, he is not under a curse. The righteousness or unrighteousness of a person cannot be unjustly imputed to another. We see then that what brings any curse/yoke is personal iniquity against God, and what breaks any curse/yoke is implicit obedience of God. The only way to love God is to implicitly obey all he has commanded us to observe to do for our own good (see

Deut. 5:29, 10:12-13, John 14:15, 23). And to love and obey God begins with the fear of Him – to depart from all evil deeds – which is the foundation of eternal life (see Job 28:28, Prov. 8:13, Eccl. 12:13). There is, therefore, no generational curse on any soul that lives and obeys God; for anointing (salvation – the knowledge of the truth) breaks the yoke and sets one free from curse (see Is. 10:27, John 8:32,36, Rom. 8:1).

It was due to man's wickedness in perpetually misinterpreting and manipulating God's commandment, that God continued painstakingly to use His prophets to attempt to correct misapplication and misinterpretation of this important commandment. As it is written in Deuteronomy, the fifth book of Moses; "Father shall not be put to death for their children, nor shall children be put to death for their fathers; a person shall be put to death for his own sin" (Deut. 24:16). Again, it is written: "Now it happened as soon as the kingdom was established in his [King Amaziah] hand, that he executed his servants who had murdered his father the king. But the children of the murderers he did not execute according to what is written in the book of the Law of Moses, in which the Lord commanded saying, "Fathers shall not be put to death for their children, nor shall children be put to death for their fathers; but a person shall be put to death for his own sin" (2 Kin. 14:5-6).

Sadly, despite this simple, clear unequivocal and unambiguous commandment of God, the children of Israel, as it is with the false prophets, teachers, and preachers of this day, continued to impute the father's iniquity to the children, due to wickedness and hardness of their hearts. Due to such unfair and unjust misapplication, misinterpretation and gross violation and abuse of His commandments, the Lord decided to do away with His first covenant for a new one. As it is written: "In those days they shall say no more: 'The fathers have eaten sour grapes, And the children's teeth are set on edge.' But every one shall die for his own iniquity; every man who eats the sour grapes, his teeth shall be set on edge. "Behold, the days are coming, says the LORD, when I will make a new covenant with the house of Israel and with the house of Judah- not according to the covenant that I made with their fathers in the day that I took them by the hand to lead them out of the land of Egypt, My covenant which they broke, though I was a husband to them, says the LORD. But this is the covenant that I will make with the house of Israel after those days, says the LORD: I will put My law in their minds, and write it on their hearts, and I will be their God, and they shall be My people. No more shall every man teach his neighbor, and every man his brother, saying, 'Know the LORD,' for they all shall know Me, from the least of them to the greatest of them, says the LORD. For I will forgive their iniquity, and their sin I will remember no more" (Jer. 31:29-34).

God's new covenant was fulfilled in His only begotten Son, Jesus Christ, who came to show the way, the truth and the life. As it is written: "But the hour is coming, and now is, when the true worshipers will worship the Father in spirit and truth; for the Father is seeking such to worship Him.

God is Spirit, and those who worship Him must worship in spirit and truth" (John 4:23-24). That God sent His firm authority in His Son, is evident, as it written: "For the wrath of God is revealed from heaven against all ungodliness and unrighteousness of men, who suppress the truth in unrighteousness, because what may be known of God is manifest in them, for God has shown it to them. For since the creation of the world His invisible attributes are clearly seen, being understood by the things that are made, even His eternal power and Godhead, so that they are without excuse..." (Rom. 1:18-20). This is a truth worthy of acceptance, anyone who is under a curse has himself, not his father or forefather to blame. Whoever hears His voice and keeps His word is not under any curse, but he is set free by the knowledge of the truth (living and being the truth) which is in the Son (truth) (see John 8:32,36).

Let us return now to the chronology of God's relentless efforts to put to rest the notion of generational curse as His general commandment. It is my considered recommendation that the reader endeavors to read very carefully, the Book of Ezekiel, chapter eighteen, verses one through twenty, wherein God strenuously stated that He never commanded generational curse. Suffice it here to cite but some verses of the said chapter. "The word of the LORD came to me again, saying, "What do you mean when you use this proverb concerning the land of Israel, saying: 'The fathers have eaten sour grapes, and the children's teeth are set on edge'? "As I live," says the Lord GOD, "you shall no longer use this proverb in Israel." Behold, all souls are

Mine; The soul of the father As well as the soul of the son is Mine; The soul who sins shall die" (Ezek. 18:1-4). Further provisions of this chapter tell us that if a just father begets a wicked son, the son, not the father shall die for his wicked deeds; and if a wicked father begets a just son, the father shall die, but the son shall live. However, where both the father and his son are wicked, they shall both die. (see Ezek. 18:5-19). The same chapter summaries as follows: "The soul who sins shall die. The son shall not bear the guilt of the father, nor the father bear the guilt of the son. The righteousness of the righteous shall be upon himself, and the wickedness of the wicked shall be upon himself. (Ezek. 18:20).

There is no mention of generational curse in the New Testament, rather new testament scriptures make it abundantly clear that whoever hears Christ's voice and obeys all He has commanded has everlasting life and not under any curse (see John 3:16-18; 5:24; Rom. 8:32,36; Rom. 8:1). But whoever rejects Christ, also rejects the Father, and is under a curse (not the father's curse), because he hates God (see Ex. 20:6; John 3:36; 1 John 2:23). Whoever does not obey His voice (truth) condemns himself (see John 3:19); and each person shall give account of his own deeds and bear his own load – not the deeds and load of his father or son (see 2 Cor. 5:10; Gal. 6:5); and each person shall be rewarded according to his own works, not the works of another (see Matt 16:27; Rev. 20:12; 22:12). As the wise preacher, would say, so it is, here then is the conclusion of this matter: In Christ Jesus, there is no generational curse – for in Him there is neither free nor slave, but new creation who have put on Christ (see

Gal. 3:26-29). In Christ Jesus, the veil of bondage is taken off, and the truth of God is put on (see 2 Cor. 3:14-16). If anyone comes to you with a contrary conclusion or doctrine, let him be accursed. You must boldly and fiercely refuse such an antichrist; for whoever receives or gives to a false prophet shall receive the false prophet's reward. As it is written: "Whoever transgresses and does not abide in the doctrine of Christ does not have God. He who abides in the doctrine of Christ has both the Father and the Son. If anyone comes to you and does not bring this doctrine, do not receive him into your house nor greet him; for he who greets him shares in his evil deeds (2 John 9-11).

I am not at all ignorant of some arguments marshaled out by hawkers and enforcers of the doctrine of generational curse to buttress their evil commercial enterprise, contrary to the expressed commandment of God. In their vigorous and malicious attempts to justify their stronghold on gullible and fearful souls, they would arrogantly and boldly cite instances in the Bible, in which God cursed families. God, in exceptional cases, and for whatever reason best known to Him, had in the past and may now or in the future dispense His punishment as it pleases Him. God is God; He does whatever pleases Him and who can strive with Him? As it is written, "Woe to him who strives with his maker." Let the potsherd strive with the potsherds of the earth! Shall the clay say to him who forms it, 'What are you making?' Or shall your handiwork say, 'He has no hands?' (Is. 45:9). However, this is the indisputable and incontrovertible fact: God never commanded or ordained generational curse – that is, God did not command the imputation of one's iniquity to another, period! And even assuming arguendo that there is a generational curse, as we have stated before, anointing breaks every yoke. Our anointing is true salvation in Christ which is the knowledge of God (the truth) – which is living and being the truth; and whoever the Son has set free is free for all purposes (see John 8:32, 36). For where the Spirit of God is there is liberty and freedom from bondage and curse; for all in Christ – that is, those who live and walk in His Spirit are new creation with all the old gone (see 2 Cor. 3:17, 5:17). One who is still under a curse is not born of the Spirit of God – not because of what his parents have done, but rather because of his own iniquity – not living a life pleasing to God always. For those who reject the truth that is in Christ hate God, and as such, they are already under condemnation (see John 3:19).

CHAPTER NINE

SAD STATE OF A COMMUNITY IN DIASPORA
– A PROFILE OF PEOPLE IN BONDAGE IN THE LAND OF LIBERTY AND FREEDOM

Peradventure and in the very likely event you bump into a black person in Houston, Texas USA – that part of the globe which is reputed for its freedom and liberty, and your uninvited acquaintance happens to be constantly looking over his own shoulder or talking of imaginary spiritual forces and enemies monitoring and trailing him, your guess may be considered and informed if it leads to the conclusion that the frightened individual is of African nationality, more likely a West, East and south African extraction. Your informed and intelligent guess may also lead you to conclude the individual either belongs to one of the many home-grown, traditionally doctrinal and doctored churches which specialize in exploiting the vulnerability and weakness of their own kind, or perhaps remotely controlled by false pastors or prophets/prophetess from far away Africa – the so-called spiritual fathers and mothers in the Lord, whose specialty is in hawking, reinforcing and feeding their victims with lies and spiritual fear of the unknown, in exchange for dollars. Of a sad fact is that the victim, like most of his brothers and sisters in his community, might have been residing in the United States of America for countless years and perhaps has achieved one of the highest levels of academic accomplishments/degrees. But how does one comprehend why such highly educated and supposedly knowledgeable individuals in the land of freedom and liberty have suddenly found themselves not only walloping in fear and darkness but allowing themselves to be easily manipulated, deceived, controlled and subjected to bondage by half-baked, self-made false pastors, prophets, and prophetess parading themselves as servants of the Most High? While some are shamelessly and remotely controlled by these false pastors, prophets and prophetess and prayer gurus from far away Africa – who feed them with fear, leading to bondage of mind, yet others are victims of some imported home grown and brewed traditional churches which are modelled after fetish doctrine, belief and satanic ritualistic practices.

Please permit me to say that I am not here speaking in terms of outright disapproval or condemnation of African churches in the United States, rather to state the obvious – the proliferation of some of these churches with their anti-Christ doctrinal belief and practices, has ushered in such an alarming and abominable number of agents of darkness, manipulation, deception, lies and idolatrous covetousness. In that by hawking, reinforcing and perpetuating spiritual fear of the unknown, they have succeeded in setting the hands of spiritual and physical progress and development clock of some of our people back to the dark stone age.

Let it be known that there are some good African based churches in the United States, but the few which preach and practice heresies like generational curses, an eye for an eye, death to their enemies, "holy ghost fire", "die by fire" against their supposed enemies, contrary to the gospel and doctrine of Jesus Christ are enemies of the cross. These are the ones who perpetuate violence against the kingdom of God and their people. They are worse than the Pharisees of Christ's time, whose evil deeds must be exposed and stopped. For they have ushered in massive influx of spiritual fear, devilish and blasphemous doctrine and practices all designed to make merchandise of their brothers and sisters. As it written: "For many walk, of whom I have told you often, and now tell you even weeping, that they are the enemies of the cross of Christ: whose end is destruction, whose god is their belly, and whose glory is in their shame—who set their mind on earthly things" (Phil. 3:18-19). Again, the apostle Peter lamenting about the roles of these false prophets, stated thus: "But there were also false prophets among the people, even as there will be false teachers among you, who will secretly bring in destructive heresies, even denying the Lord who bought them, and bring upon themselves swift destruction. And many will follow their destructive ways, because of whom the way of truth will be blasphemed. By covetousness they will exploit you with deceptive words; for a long time their judgment has not been idle, and their destruction does not slumber" (2 Pet. 2:1-3). Again he (Peter) stated the obvious: "While they promise them liberty, [ritualistic deliverance and liberation] they themselves are slaves of corruption; for by whom a person is overcome, by him also he is brought into bondage" (2 Pet 2:19). The apostle Paul emphatically stated that such false prophets must be stopped. "For there are many insubordinate, both idle talkers and deceivers, especially those of the circumcision, whose mouths must be stopped, who subvert whole households, teaching things which they ought not, for the sake of dishonest gain" (Titus 1:10-11).

The scripture says that while knowledge increases power, people do perish for lack of it (see Prov. 24:5, Hos. 4:6). We know and believe that knowledge of the truth of God is eternal life – knowledge of God is the implicit obedience of every word of His which is what sets us free from the domain of darkness and bondage (see John 8:32. 17:3; 1 John

2:3-5). The truth is that light that shines in the darkness, and yet darkness does not comprehend it (see John 1:5). What do we then say of people who are supposed to know or should have known the truth and yet, due to itching ears, invite deceivers and manipulators to put them in bondage? Even our hope for a changed society —our children, the ones we should raise unto God as a generation of gods, are encouraged and pushed by their enslaved parents to submit to these agents of deception and darkness. Some of these innocent and free children are being told and made to believe by these evil agents that they need deliverance from some spirits trailing, stalking and stagnating them – some ancestral spirit or those remotely sent from their parents' African villages, by relations, usually uncles. Some are told that their fortunes are being tied by their relations, as such they would necessarily need deliverance – deliverance may include, but not limited to drinking some incantations to either vomit or neutralize the imaginary evil. Some are made to believe that any adverse health issue they may have is because of a generational curse or evil spell, which must be cast out and returned to the sender – popularly labeled 'return to sender' – a common practice by fetish priests.

It is generally believed that a society is better the more its population is educated, but today we are witnessing a sad reversal of any gain we had ever made in the past – a rapid dimming of our light before our very eyes – the villain being the very institution (church) that is supposed, commissioned to set the captive free. The said institution is now at the helm of enslavement, captivity, exploitation, extortion and bondage. I have had numerous conversations with the most educated elites of some African countries and was left speechless at the level of decimation of minds because of the evil deeds of some leaders of churches. Sadly, my people seem to relish their enslavement. As it is written: "An astonishing and horrible thing has been committed in the land: The prophets prophesy falsely, and the priests rule by their own power, and My people love to have it so. But what will you do in the end" (Jer. 5:30-31)? For as it is with the theory of economy of demand and supply, so it is with those who kindle fire and their accomplices who supply the firewood (see Prov. 26:20). As it written by the apostle Paul in his second epistle to the Corinthians: "For you put up with it if one brings you into bondage, if one devours you, if one takes from you, if one exalts himself, if one strikes you on the face" (2 Cor. 11:20). For some strange truth, the crowd appears to flock to those who deceive them with empty "feel good" words, earthly miracles, signs and wonders, devoid of eternal value - while the undiluted truth of God is despised. The reason for such unfortunate trend is obvious – those whose deeds are evil tend to love the ways of darkness. As it is written: "And this is the condemnation, that the light has come into the world, and men loved darkness rather than light because their deeds were evil. For everyone practicing evil hates the light and does not come to the light, lest his deeds should be exposed" (John 3:19-20). Sadly, due to faulty, or shaky, or wrong spiritual foundation upon which most of us are building our spiritual walk/life, we lack understanding of what it means to be established and rooted firmly in God's undiluted truth – implicit obedience which is our shield against all forms of malicious deception, manipulation, lies and spiritual bondage. Although, while it is certainly true that God loves all and His mercies endure forever, because God endures forever, yet we must understand that God loves those who love Him (see Prov. 8:17); and He remains with us if we are with Him – but if we forsake or deny Him, He will forsake and deny us (see 2 Chr. 15:2; 2 Tim 2:11-13). As it is written: "Therefore whoever hears these sayings of Mine, and does them, I will liken him to a wise man who built his house on the rock: and the rain descended, the floods came, and the winds blew and beat upon that house; and it did not fall, for it was founded on the rock. But everyone who hears these sayings of Mine, and does not do them, will be like a foolish man who built his house on the sand: and the rain descended, the floods came, and the winds blew and beat upon that house, and it fell. And great was its fall" (Matt 7:24-27).

A crucial question is how do we avoid and resist being put into bondage by agents of darkness.

CHAPTER TEN

PATHETIC STORIES / TESTIMONIES OF MINDS IN BONDAGE

If you have not yet heard of incidents of people in the United states of America, who are under constant spiritual monitoring surveillance, or being chased by birds or some spiritual objects of prey, please bear with me for a moment, and lend me your ears to hear pathetic stories and testimonies of enslaved and unsound minds in the land of freedom and liberty. All the sad stories/testimonies written below are based on true experiences and encounters. They lead to conclusive evidence that most of our people, among them are the most educated and oldest residents of their community, are simply wallowing in darkness and fear, having mortgaged their knowledge and experience to the tight and manipulative grip of agents of the devil, parading themselves as servants of God. They are sadly made to believe emphatically that their lives and fortune are being tied and monitored by relations and some evil spirits from far away Africa, who are opposed to their continuing existence and success. Despite their high educational accomplishments and extensive exposure to a free culture, yet they willingly invite and allow these false prophets, pastors, and "prayer warriors" to control and destroy their lives.

Some have confided in me their fear to visit their homes in Africa because their pastors, or prophets/prophetess, or prayer warriors had warned them that their compounds in Africa had been mined with dangerous charms, designed to kill them and their families, should they dare to set foot there, without first undergoing some ritualistic deliverance or cleansing. Most of the victims of this scam have confessed that they sheepishly expended huge sums of money for such worthless exercises. Some of the victims, who have resided in the United States for many years without visiting their African homes, send money almost on a monthly period to these agents of darkness, ostensibly for the liberation of their families and land – just imagine, land liberation!

Some have been robbed of the joy of living and faith in God, having yielded to voices of fear, apprehension, suspicion, superstition, bitterness, anxiety and depression. One victim was rendered to fear her own shadow – even afraid to venture outside her house because she believed her pastor, who told her that a bird of prey was sent from her village in Africa to chase, hurt, haunt, and torment her in the United

States of America. Well, after spending all her savings, her condition has so deteriorated that she now finds home in a psychiatric ward.

There was a case of one who saw a tiny snake in his garage, and rather than kill or remove the snake, he ran terrified to his bedroom, where he embarked on endless and repetitious screaming of "blood of Jesus," while the poor snake got away. Our brother regained his senses enough to call his prophet in Africa, who told him that he had just encountered a bad omen which would require special prayers, in addition to sowing of seed. Our brother did as he was instructed; and at the end of it all, after expending huge sums of money on worthless rituals and seed sowing, he had nothing but a worthless bottle of olive oil to show for it. And even the so-called "anointed oil" came with its ritualistic instructions – he was to drink some of the content every other three days, and sprinkle some in front of his house, in addition to rubbing same all over his body, when he decided to go to bed, or outside his house. Further, he was, like most victims, prescribed some doses of scriptural readings, most of which are lifted from the Book of Psalms.

Let me make it clear that I have nothing against anointing oil; for the Bible allows elders of churches to pray for the sick, "anointing him with oil in the name of the Lord" (see James 5:14). However, it is an abominable astonishment how the devourers of the Lord's flock (false prophets/prophetess, pastors, and prayer warriors) have turned olive oil into god of their victims. Some (victims) dare not leave their homes, or travel without their "anointed oil." Worse still, these deceivers have turned olive oil into one of the most demanded and costly commodities. And astonishingly, these imposters of God's servants charge hefty sums of money for the oil.

I had witnessed astonishing horror in many churches in Africa and the United States, where the so-called G.O. (General Overseer), shamelessly told all in the congregation to schedule deliverance sessions with his staff, because "all of you are under some human and spiritual attacks;" and amazingly, members of his congregation sheepishly obliged. One visiting General Overseer from Africa told his captive audience in the United States, that whatever health issue they had was due to generational curse, or remotely sent by their relations in Africa. The echo of the one word "Amen" by misled members of that congregation, still haunts and terrifies me.

Do you know that there is hardly any family that is spared the divisive evil of false prophets and deliverers? Painfully, many young women are at odd with their own mothers, because their prophets/prophetess, pastors and prayer warriors told them that their (victims') mothers are witches, whose specialty is to "steal the fetus from their wombs." Rather than comforting and encouraging some unfortunate women, these agents of darkness make them believe that their barrenness or miscarriage is due to witchcraft, or evil persons, or spirit, who has vowed to rob them of the joy of motherhood.

Some were told to sow "sufficient seed" for special prayers of appeasement to gods that have withheld, or blocked, or tied their fortune. This is true and worthy of acceptance, if any has his "fortune tied" by another person or spirit, he is yet to be born of God; for where the Spirit of God is there is freedom and liberty (see 2 Cor. 3:17). Even assuming for argument only that this ridiculous assertion has any credit to it, who can harm one who is a true follower of God (see 1 Pet. 3:13)?

Many now rely on their favorite "book of dreams," authored by these false prophets, to give them the underlying spiritual interpretation of their dreams. Most of these people are now ruled by dreams of every size and shape. There are some books detailing interpretation of evil sounds of birds and other animals.

Some told me that they were made to attend special mountain prayers and sacrifices in Houston, Texas – did you get that – mountains in Houston, Texas, U.S.A! You will agree with me that these deceivers have a bizarre twist to their manipulative enterprise. These agents of darkness have descended on their vulnerable brothers and sisters, in quest of money. But for those who hear, we know who made the last sacrifice; and the same told us that the hour has come when true worshippers will no longer worship in Jerusalem or on the mountains, but rather in truth and spirit, within them (see John 4:21-24).

I must confess that all that is written above is merely a tip of the iceberg of the horrors of false prophets/prophetess, pastors and prayer warriors. Time, space, and scope will not permit me to detail more pathetic stories of minds in bondage – that will require many volumes. But then, what can we say about the darkness that has paralyzed any spiritual light in many nations of Africa, particularly, West, East and South African countries, where false prophets and pastors run wild and dangerous. These countries now experience spiritual fear on a devastating level, fueled by these enemies of the body of Christ. Driven by covetousness, they have wickedly succeeded in getting people to believe in the devil; they are credited with instigating and facilitating stupid and ungodly strife, discord, conflict, suspicion, and distrust in just about every Christian family in these countries; they will not stop until they convince every beautiful or fairly skinned young lady that she is being haunted by a spiritual marine husband; and in guise of delivering their victims from the grip of evil spirits, they conduct bush prayers, where they subject them to both physical and spiritual abuse. In some instances, these false prophets had told their victims that the enemies after their lives were their own children. How wicked can that be?

All those who manipulate, deceive, lie, abuse and take undue advantage of vulnerable children of God have reserved their place in hell, except they repent, renounce and forsake their abominable ways. The abuse of God's children under color of authority of priesthood/pastor hood, or calling, in the name of the Lord, as the two sons of Eli did, is an abomination of epic proportion in His sight (see 1 Sam. 2:22-36). As it is written: Then, the Lord said to Samuel, "Behold,

I will do something in Israel at which both ears of everyone who hears it will tingle. In that day I will perform against Eli all that I have spoken concerning his house, from beginning to end. For I have told him that I will judge his house forever for the iniquity which he knows, because his sons made themselves vile, and he did not restrain them. And therefore I have sworn to the house of Eli that the iniquity of Eli's house shall not be atoned for by sacrifice or offering forever" (1 Sam. 3:11-14). I strongly believe that God mercifully set the Eli example for our own admonishment. And if this unchangeable God refused Moses entry to the promised land, what do these present generation preachers think they are? If God did not spare Moses and the angels who rebelled against Him, He would not spare us either, except we repent and forsake our evil ways TODAY (see Deut. 3:23-28; 1 Cor. 10:1-12; 2 Pet. 2:1-6; Jude 1-7).

CHAPTER ELEVEN

DEVASTATING CONSEQUENCES OF SPIRITUAL FEAR OF THE UNKNOWN

It is an indisputable fact that fear, especially spiritual fear of the unknown, is one of the most horrendous tormentors of a person; and to a great extent, it causes one to lose total control of one's mind and dignity. Spiritual fear of the unknown robs one of all dignity, self-confidence, peace and joy of life. The victim lives in self-imposed prison without walls; for spiritual fear of the unknown knows no boundary, causing its victim to live in an imaginary world of suspicion, apprehension, uncertainty and superstition. Most often, a victim of spiritual fear of the unknown finds himself in his own solitary confinement or seclusion, thereby exposing him to more vulnerability to false and scam prophets, besides his susceptibility to serious physical ailments, including but not limited to depression, constant headache, insomnia, anxiety disorder, weakness and nervous breakdown. Spiritual fear of the unknown simply erodes and zaps one's confidence as well as robs one of the joy and meaning of daily living. A victim of spiritual fear is constantly on edge, afraid of even his own shadow. He is as a haunted person who flees at the sound of a fallen leaf. As it is written: "The wicked flee when no one pursues, But the righteous are bold as a lion" (Prov. 28:1). Spiritual fear of the unknown is a constant tormentor of its victims; it is a major catalyst of faintness of heart, which renders its victims powerless to stand against the enemy. Usually, it pushes its victim into premature surrender, even before the battle begins.

It is quite evident that one who is in bondage of spiritual fear of the unknown is yet to know God – he is yet to be made one with God or His truth. One who is born of His Spirit is a spirit, and if born of His Spirit, he is led by His Spirit, and is therefore god, even unto the devil. Those led by His Spirit are spirits (children of God; these know the truth and are set free by the Spirit of truth and liberty); the evil one cannot touch them (see John 1:12, 13, 3:5-6, 8:32,36; Rom. 8:9,14; 1 John 5:18). The only way to know God is to obey Him implicitly – that is eternal life (see John 8:55, 17:3, 1 John 2:3-5). The knowledge of the truth of God – that is, living and being the truth, shall set one free (see John 8:32). Whoever knows God is perfect in love for God and all people, and perfect love, we have read, casts out fear (see 1 John 4:7,8 16-18).

Those who are spiritually fearful of the unknown are truly in bondage – no liberty or freedom – they are slaves of the unknown. As it is written: "Now the Lord is the Spirit; and where the Spirit of the Lord is, there is liberty" (2 Cor. 3:17). This leads us to the obvious conclusion that whoever is in bondage of spiritual fear does not have the Spirit of God. And because the victim of spiritual fear does not have liberty, he also lacks sound mind – for God has not given us the spirit of fear but of sound mind (see 2 Tim. 1:7); and if of unsound mind, he is still an unbeliever, who is wallowing in the uselessness of his mind (see Eph. 4:17,18). One cannot worship or serve God in truth while he is in bondage. When we cannot worship, or serve God in spirit and truth, there is obviously, another we serve – the devil. Those who are in bondage of spiritual fear of the unknown believe in the devil; for if we live in fear of the devil, it means we believe in his works, so much so that our belief causes us to tremble and faint before him. We believe in one whom we believe his works, and we are afraid of one who is stronger than we are. As it is written: "Believe Me that I am in the Father and the Father in Me, or else believe Me for the sake of the works themselves" (John 14:11).

For those who are spiritually fearful of the unknown, the coming of the Lord, Jesus Christ (death and resurrection) is in vain for them, since they are still not released from the fear of death. As it is written in the Epistle to the Hebrews: "Inasmuch then as the children have partaken of flesh and blood, He Himself likewise shared in the same, that through death He might destroy him who had the power of death, that is, the devil, and release those who through fear of death were all their lifetime subject to bondage" (Heb. 2:14-15).

The devil's greatest weapon is fear, and one cannot fight the enemy with his own weapon. Our weapon is mighty in God, who emphatically warns us not to fear, for He is with us (see Is. 41:1-13). The billion-dollar question is, are we with God – for He is with those who are fully with Him in implicit obedience (see 2 Chr. 15:2; 2 Tim. 2:11-13)? It is certainly true that nothing can separate us from His love and cover, except we – for our iniquity separates us from Him (see Is. 59:2; Rom. 8:38, 39). Therefore, let us remember the "IF" factor – if we are in Him and He is in us, nothing can harm us or be against us, because He is the greater in us than are all the forces in the world (see Luke 10:19; Rom. 8:31; 1 Pet. 3:13; 1 John 4:4). Therefore, we proclaim in vain that no weapon formed against us shall prosper when our hearts are far from God; we plead his blood, rather than drink it: and we declare our heart out what we do not have because of our rebellion. But let us seek God and His righteousness, and His full hedge will be ours.

The most severe consequence of spiritual fear of the unknown is the spiritual death of its victim. One who is in bondage of spiritual fear has little or no faith in the supremacy of His God and that all power over life and death belongs to Him. Having little or no faith gives birth to suspicion and superstitious belief, which in turn gives birth to unsound mind. Unsound mind begets fear of the unknown, which in turn leads to itching ears; itching ear begets vulnerability and gullibility, which is a fertile ground for vultures, dogs and devouring wolves in sheep clothing. Once this advanced stage is reached, delusive spirits take over the victim, prompting him to yearn for, seek and believe in many confusing voices and lies; and when it is fully matured or convinced, it leads to death. Here is how our spiritual fear map looks like:

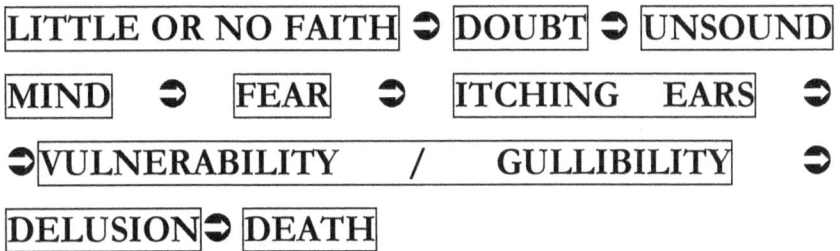

LITTLE OR NO FAITH ➲ DOUBT ➲ UNSOUND MIND ➲ FEAR ➲ ITCHING EARS ➲ ➲VULNERABILITY / GULLIBILITY ➲ DELUSION➲ DEATH

When one reaches the delusive state, he is simply perishing, as he begins to rely on, and trust more in false prophets, with their dazzling demonic signs and lying wonders. As it is written: "The coming of the lawless one is according to the working of Satan, with all power, signs, and lying wonders, and with all unrighteous deception among those who perish, because they did not receive the love of the truth, that they might be saved. And for this reason, God will send them strong delusion, that they should believe the lie, that they all may be condemned who did not believe the truth but had pleasure in unrighteousness" (2 Thess. 2:9-12).

CHAPTER TWELVE

HOW TO ELIMINATE GULLIBILITY AND RESIST AGENTS OF BONDAGE

The scripture tells us that to be free from, especially spiritual enslavement and bondage, one must necessarily know the truth (see John 8:32). To know the truth is to know God and to know God is to live and implicitly obey Him (see John 8:55; 14:15; 1 John 2:3-5). In other words, to know the truth is to be the truth – and to be the truth is to live it - that is becoming one with the truth by abiding in His word and His word abiding in us – this is exactly what it means to eat and drink His blood and flesh (see John 6:53-56, 8:31, 15:4-7). We believe whoever is made free by the knowledge of the truth in Christ, is free indeed (see John 8:36). This belief has informed my conclusion that whoever is deceived or put in bondage of spiritual fear of the unknown is simply because he is not the truth, or the light which darkness and its agents cannot comprehend. As it is written: "Now the Lord is the Spirit; and where the Spirit of the Lord is, there is liberty (2 Cor. 3:17). It, therefore, holds true that where there is bondage, the Spirit of God is not there; and if the Spirit of God is not in us, it means we have no truth (God) in us. And without God's hedge/armor, one is at the mercy of demonic agents and forces, as they maliciously roam around looking for victims/preys.

My people must take heed how, what, when, and where they hear the word of God – for many, I say, seek God in all the wrong places, yet God is near at any point of every breath we take – only that we must seek Him with all that is within us, if we desire to find Him (see Jer. 29:13). The only way to seek God is to renounce, depart, and forsake all our sinful, evil deeds. As it is written: "Seek the LORD while He may be found, call upon Him while He is near. Let the wicked forsake his way, and the unrighteous man his thoughts; Let him return to the LORD, And He will have mercy on him; and to our God, For He will abundantly pardon" (Is. 55:6-7). This is the only way to merge on His highway of freedom and liberty; it is the only way to begin a meaningful intimate relationship with God.

It is imperative to make haste to understand that a relationship with God that sets one free is not about religion, church or denominational doctrine – but rather an intimate relationship requiring perfection of fear of Him (depart from evil deeds), leading to implicit obedience, which in turn leads to righteousness and holiness, which is the hallmark of total transformation of the heart, mind, body and spirit. This is the new creation – born of God – spirits of God on earth – able to live and forgive even the worst enemies and able to obey all His commandments – thereby setting themselves free from man's bondage, having been clothed with the whole armor of God (see Ezek. 11:19-20; 36:26-27; Matt. 5:43-48; John 3:5-6; 4:23-24; 2 Cor. 5:17; Gal. 3:27; Eph. 4:24; 6:11-17). It is certainly when we wholly/fully submit to God, by doing what He requires of us, in strict accordance with His prescribed rules, that we can successfully eliminate our vulnerability and resist agents of bondage (see 2 Cor. 10:3-6; Eph. 6:11-17; 2 Tim. 2:5; James 4:7; 1 John 5:18). The sum of the above is that one is set free when he knows (lives) the truth of the undiluted and uncompromising word of Jesus Christ our Savior.

For one to successfully resist agents of bondage, he must necessarily resist himself first. I know and acknowledge that I am my greatest weakness and worst enemy, which must be dealt with first before looking outward. It is indeed a fact that the things we do lead us to temptations which open wide doors for agents of bondage to exploit. As it is written by the apostle James, "Let no one say when he is tempted, "I am tempted by God"; for God cannot be tempted by evil, nor does He Himself tempt anyone. But each one is tempted when he is drawn away by his own desires and enticed. Then, when desire has conceived, it gives birth to sin; and sin, when it is full-grown, brings forth death" (James 1:13-15). At the heart or our weakness and enmity is a lack of genuine and perfect love for God and all people. We have read that God is perfect love and that we ought to be perfect in loving others as He is, that is if we seriously intend to walk with Him; because as we have read, perfect love neutralizes all fear. "You have heard that it was said, 'YOU SHALL LOVE YOUR NEIGHBOR and hate your enemy.' But I say to you, love your enemies, bless those who curse you, do good to those who hate you, and pray for those who spitefully use you and persecute you" (Matt. 5:43-44). Perfect love distinguishes us as true children of God (gods); for God is love – and we ought to be as He is, for two cannot walk together except they have meeting of the mind (see Amos 3:3: Matt. 5:45-48; 1 John 4:7, 8, 11, 12, 17-21). When we are perfect in love, we will arm ourselves with the most potent weapon against the devil, his agents, and weapon of his enslavement. One who hates any human being hates God; the only way to love God is to love others and implicitly obey Him. Our Lord says that the only way to demonstrate our love for Him is to obey all He has commanded us, just as He obeyed the Father who sent Him (see John 8:29; 14:15, 23; 15:14). As it is further written: "If someone says, "I love God," and hates his brother, he is a liar; for he who does not love his brother whom he has seen, how can he love God whom he has not seen?" (1 John 4:20).

So I say to all who have ears to hear, put on the whole armor of the truth (perfect love and implicit obedience) so that you may be able to resist the devil and his agents; and in addition, put on the whole armor of love in order to eliminate your gullibility and vulnerability – so that when a false prophet comes with enslaving words of prophecy and sorcery, you can resist him with the heart of love and goodness which mitigates against unreasonable and unsubstantiated suspicion. And even if there is any truth to any case, as I am not naïve and oblivious of the fact that evil and wicked forces lurk around every corner of the world, yet our victory is assured in God (one with Him), who is the weapon of warfare of the righteous; and the only way to obtain righteousness is through implicit obedience, which is not possible without perfect love (see John 16:33; Rom. 6:16, 8:31; 2 Cor. 10:3-6; Eph. 6:11-13; 1 Pet. 3:13). I strongly recommend that the reader fully reads and digests the Epistle of the apostle Paul to the Ephesians, Chapter 6, versus 14-18, for an understanding of the prescribed ways to obtain and keep God's whole armor against the devil. Finally, and more importantly, our greatest authority is Jesus Christ, the ultimate Word who came from the Father and one with the Father – none greater will ever come; He is the only way, the truth, and the life; His word is spirit and life; and none can snatch His out of His hands (see John 1: 1-5, 10:28-30, 14:6,). Therefore, whoever earnestly desires to eliminate gullibility, and resist false prophets, deceivers, and manipulators, let him abide fully and always in the word of Jesus Christ. We will hear His voice if we are His, and the voice of false prophets we will always shun.

CHAPTER THIRTEEN

THE TWO KEYS OF FREEDOM AND LIBERTY

There are two indispensable and all-important and exclusive keys of the kingdom of God – Love and Obedience. The kingdom of God – the only permanent peace, rest and freedom - is about an intimate relationship with God and fellow human beings. The kingdom of God is anchored on these two keys; the character of God is defined by them; and where any of them is absent, God is not there. They are the specific keys our Lord came down from heaven to establish – the way, the truth, and the life. Therefore, all those who are truly born of the Spirit of God are born into perfect love and obedience – which is the kingdom of God within them, by the knowledge of the truth, which is the perfection of these two keys. To know these keys is to know God – which is eternal life; the only way to know the two keys is to live them always; the only way to live them is to love God and others, and the only way to love God is to obey Him.

> As it is written: "And this is eternal life, that they may know You, the only true God, and Jesus Christ whom You have sent" (John 17:3). "If you love Me, keep My commandments" (John 14:15). "If anyone loves Me, he will keep My word; and My Father will love him, and We will come to him and make Our home with him" (John 14:23). "Now by this, we know that we know Him, if we keep His commandments. He who says, "I know Him," and does not keep His commandments, is a liar, and the truth is not in him. But whoever keeps His word, truly the love of God is perfected in him. By this, we know that we are in Him" (1 John 2:3-5).

One striking obstacle to peace and freedom of mind is our imperfection of love for other human beings (all) created in God's image. In most cases, we simply erroneously labor in our own assumption that our desire to please or love God is sufficiently independent of love for others as God loves us. This amounts to false living; for if we do not love others as God loves us, we neither love God, nor are we of Him – for God is perfect love – and His children are commanded to be perfect in love as He is (see Matt. 5:48; 1 John 2:6; 4:7). As it is written: "A new commandment I give to you, that you love one another; as I have loved you, that you also love one another. By this, all will know that you are My disciples, if you have love for one another" (John 13:34-35). Again, "But he who hates his brother is in darkness and walks in darkness, and does not know where he is going because the darkness has blinded his eyes" (1 John 2:11).

Therefore, one who is a victim of bondage of spiritual fear is not only in thick darkness, but enslaved and imprisoned within himself without physical walls. The perfection of the two keys of the kingdom of God removes the scales and the potent spell off the eyes of the victim; it is the source of victorious and free living, even over and above those real, perceived and imagined enemies and "overwhelming giants", who were supposedly born to torment us perpetually. Even of more significant value, it sets you free from the choking and strangling hold of devouring agents of falsehood, deception, manipulation, lies and fear. As it is written: "When a man's ways please the LORD, He makes even his enemies to be at peace with him" (Prov. 16:7). "The evil will bow before the good, and the wicked at the gates of the righteous" (Prov. 14:19).

AVENGE NOT – FORGIVE ALL AND AVENGE NOT

Whatever you do, if you desire to be free from bondage and enter the kingdom of God, flee from taking vengeance, or even an appearance of it. To heed this caveat will keep you and your family from the cyclical saga of fear and death. From Genesis to Revelation, God commands that His children should never take matters into their hands by avenging themselves of evil deeds against them. Vengeance of any kind belongs exclusively to God; and anyone who takes vengeance against another reproaches God who will not fail to recompense the avenger many folds (see Deut.

Dr. Emeka O. Ozurumba

32:35; Ezek. 25:12-17). We read that although God cursed Cain for murdering his brother Abel, yet He forbade any to avenge his (Abel) death. "Therefore, whoever kills Cain, vengeance shall be taken on him sevenfold" (Gen. 4:15). This is the commandment of our God: "You shall not take vengeance, nor bear any grudge against the children of your people" (Lev. 19:18).

Therefore, vengeance of any kind, including but not limited to physical retaliation and dangerous/evil prayers – like "Holy Ghost fire," "die by fire," "return to sender," "let my enemies die," "suffer not the witch to live," is inconsistent and incompatible with the Spirit of Christ, who said, "You have heard that it was said, 'AN EYE FOR AN EYE AND A TOOTH FOR A TOOTH.' But I tell you not to resist an evil person. But whoever slaps you on your right cheek, turn the other to him also (Matt. 5:38-39). Again "You have heard that it was said, 'YOU SHALL LOVE YOUR NEIGHBOR and hate your enemy.' But I say to you, love your enemies, bless those who curse you, do good to those who hate you, and pray for those who spitefully use you and persecute you" (Matt. 5:43-44).

Consistent with the Lord and Master, the apostles and disciples of Christ adhered to this commandment of life and freedom as follows: "Repay no one evil for evil. Have regard for good things in the sight of all men" (Rom. 12:17). "Beloved, do not avenge yourselves, but rather give place to wrath; for it is written, "VENGEANCE IS MINE, I WILL REPAY," says the Lord" (Rom. 12:19). "But if you bite and devour one another, beware lest you be consumed by one another!" (Gal. 5:15). "See that no one renders evil for evil

90

to anyone, but always pursue what is good both for yourselves and for all" (1 Thess. 5:15). "Finally, all of you be of one mind, having compassion for one another; love as brothers, be tenderhearted, be courteous; not returning evil for evil or reviling for reviling, but on the contrary blessing, knowing that you were called to this, that you may inherit a blessing" (1 Pet. 3:8-9).

The above commandment is the prescribed way of God for His children – the way leading to victorious living, devoid of fear and its torment. It is the only method to cut off occasion for the devil. For if we avenge ourselves, we commit greater evil – vengeance is usually executed with a spiteful heart, with intent on causing maximum hurt or destruction; and whoever commits any form of evil is an evil and a wicked person. As it is written: "As righteousness leads to life, so he who pursues evil pursues it to his own death" (Prov. 11:19). Again, "tribulation and anguish, on every soul of man who does evil, ----" (Rom. 2:9). Evil deed can never be good; as the saying goes, "Two wrongs cannot make a right," Instead of resolving a matter, retaliation/vengeance will complicate and compound it, thereby ushering in a cyclical saga of curse and consuming death. While being pursued by the men of Joab (King David's commander), Abner, the commander of King Saul's army called to Joab and said, "Shall the sword devour forever? Do you not know that it will be bitter in the latter end? How long will it be then until you tell the people to return from pursuing their brethren?" (2 Sam. 2:26).

Since vengeance begets greater vengeance, one who engages in such evil is of the devil; he will never escape the bondage of fear or the choking yoke of fake prophets, deceivers, and manipulators; and unless he departs from his destructive path, he and his family may never know the light and peace of life.

FORGIVENESS

Forgiveness – complete and total forgiveness of all evil doers against you is the necessary and quickest recipe for freedom and liberty. You cannot avoid vengeance except you forgive all, as quickly as you can.

Love is to God as forgiveness is to love. Therefore, God is perfect love; and love is imperfect without forgiveness. If there remains a trace of bitterness and unforgiving spirit in our heart, we will never be free. Forgiveness, therefore, sets you and the offender free from bondage and anguish. We must forgive from the depths of our heart all persons who have in any way or manner hurt us; and we must forgive as often as we are offended (see Matt. 6:14-15; Matt. 18:22; Mark 11:25).

Unforgiving spirit puts you and the offender in perpetual bondage. It is a sin, a deadly form of witchcraft that eats up both the offender and the offended. Take a moment and imagine what happens to your nerves and spirit when you come face to face with the one you hold grudges against. Even the mere thought of him or the mention of his name raises your pulse and makes your blood boil, and even merely seeing or hearing what belongs to him turns you the wrong way. And pray to God that you do not remember this enemy right before you retire for the night. You see, complete forgiveness eliminates suspicion, fear, anguish and torment. Besides, God says that if we do not forgive fellow human beings, He will not forgive us. "For if you forgive men their trespasses, your heavenly Father will also forgive you. But if you do not forgive men their trespasses, neither will your Father forgive your trespasses" (Matt. 6:14-15). As many as do not have forgiving, compassionate, and merciful spirit are not led by His Spirit, and therefore, not His. The most devastating consequence of unforgiving heart is that God will retract His forgiveness of our trespasses if we refuse to forgive others who trespass against us. By refusing to forgive we willingly lead ourselves into temptation, thereby delivering ourselves to the evil one (see Matt. 6:12- 15, 18:27-35; Rom. 8:9,14; Col. 3:13). It is, therefore, prudent for us not to suffer double jeopardy because of our unforgiving heart.

RECONCILIATION -PURSUE PEACE WITH ALL PEOPLE

As many as are true disciples of Jesus Christ are commanded to do the works He did – walk as He walked. He came to show the way to the Father's kingdom, and He did so as an example for us to emulate. We are to be imitators of Him, as true disciples (Christians) of His. We are therefore to love, forgive, reconcile, and obey as He did, failure which we are not of Him (see John 13:15, 34, 35, 14:12, 15:12, 13; Col. 3:13; Eph. 5:1; 1 John 2:6; 1 Pet. 2:21). The Lord painfully reconciled us to the Father – that very single most important feat marked the fulfillment of His mission on earth. And we ought to fulfill His commission by reconciling others to Him through us; for this cause, He has given us the ministry of reconciliation. One may quickly argue that our commission/ministry of reconciliation refers to 'evangelism,' that is, making Him known to others. But how can we get others to know Him when we do not actually know Him? We are His light for others to see Him through us. For two can only walk together when they agree, and a bad tree cannot produce good fruits. If irreconciliation with others is found in our hearts, we have not forgiven them, and as such, we are disqualified from reconciling others to Him (see Amos 3:3; Matt. 5:48; 7:17, 18).

A true disciple (Christian - transformed/ born of God's Spirit) does not only have the mind of Christ (a spiritual mind set only on above), but the mind that was in Him (humble, implicit obedience, and unreserved submission). But how many of us are willing to walk as Christ walked? How many of us are prepared to lay aside the heavy weight of stupid pride of life, to become true fools for His kingdom? If there remains pride of life in us, we are yet to die from the weakness of the flesh? How many of us are willing to die that others may live in, and for Christ? Christ first reconciled us to Himself before He could do the same to the Father. As it is written: "Greater love has no one than this than to lay down one's life for his friends" (John 15:13). This is the way we demonstrate our love for one another as He has loved us (see John 15:12). As it is also written: "Most assuredly, I say to you unless a grain of wheat falls to the ground and dies, it remains alone; but if it dies, it produces much grain" (John 12:24).

We are also commanded to pursue and make peace with all. As it is written: "Pursue peace with all people, and holiness, without which no one will see the Lord: looking carefully lest anyone fall short of the grace of God, lest any root of bitterness springing up cause trouble, and by this many be defiled" (Heb. 12:14, 15). The scripture also warns us to not only pursue peace but seek it, if we seriously desire to enter God's rest (see Ps. 34:11-14). We have read that peacemakers for the kingdom's sake are true children of God (see Matt. 5:9).

Forgiveness is incomplete without sincere and godly efforts to reconcile and make peace, for both forgiveness and reconciliation are inseparable twin acts of mercy; the merciful shall obtain mercy when he needs it, and believe me, we are always in need of God's mercy (see Matt. 5:7). It is certainly true that we cannot acquire pure heart if we harden our heart and refuse to extend mercy as a token of appreciation for His mercy toward us. But whoever does not show mercy, judgment will be executed against him without mercy. As it is written: "For judgment is without mercy to the one who has shown no mercy. Mercy triumphs over judgment" (James 2:13).

CHAPTER FOURTEEN

BEWARE OF FALSE PROPHETS, PASTORS, PRIESTS, PREACHERS, ETC

Oh! My heart within me mourns for the bastardization of the truth of our God by agents of darkness within the body of Christ. My considered opinion, based on substantial and indisputable evidence, is that there has never been a more evil time than the time we are presently in; what, with millions of false prophets (prophets, prophetess, pastors, preachers, bishops, etc.) running all over the globe, deceiving and being deceived – for when one deceives others, he deceives himself first. There has never been such a time before now, when enemies within the so-called body of Christ have betrayed and blasphemed the name of God, for their pecuniary and immediate gratification – so much betrayal, heresy and blasphemy, that some leaders of leading denominations openly and boldly adopt contrary positions against God, by redefining and approving what God in the Holy Bible has adjudged an abomination to Him. All these they do for covetous gain.

I dare say that the level of mass covetous manipulation, deception, prosperity, feel good and lying wonders of these enemies of the cross, would make true prophets of the old to roll over in their graves in protest. As it is written by Jeremiah, the prophet: "My heart within me is broken because of the prophets; All my bones shake. I am like a drunken man, and like a man whom wine has overcome, because of the LORD, and because of His holy words. For the land is full of adulterers; For because of a curse, the land mourns. The pleasant places of the wilderness are dried up. Their course of life is evil, And their might *is* not right. "For both prophet and priest are profane; Yes, in My house I have found their wickedness," says the LORD" (Jer. 23:9-11).

Now, where do I begin and stop to tell of the abominable and ungodly preaching and practices which have brought almost total spiritual blindness, bondage and delusion to the children of God, especially in developing nations, where false prophecy coated with feel good and prosperity doctrine is a great booming business, with instant gestation period. And what with all the enticing, crafty, covetous and manipulative devices and schemes employed by these agents of darkness, whose gods are their belly? These wicked and heartless agents succeed in getting God's children (their true captive audience) to resist God's uncompromising and undiluted truth, and accept man's doctrine and bondage, while they make merchandise of them, devouring the vulnerable and the poor, with appetizing promises of earthly vanity. As it is written: "Because from the least of them even to the greatest of them, Everyone is given to covetousness; And from the prophet even to the priest, Everyone deals falsely. They have also healed the hurt of My people slightly, Saying, 'Peace, peace!' When there is no peace. Were they ashamed when they had committed abomination? No! They were not at all ashamed; Nor did they know how to blush. Therefore they shall fall among those who fall; At the time I punish them, They shall be cast down," says the LORD." (Jer. 6:13-15)

As the Lord told me, all "feel good," and prosperity preachers are liars because they do not present and interpret the word of God wholly, truthfully and faithfully. It is generally true that even ninety-nine percent (99%) truth is a lie – my definition of a lie being whatever that is devoid of wholesome/complete truth. Therefore, any message from the pulpit which does not have eternal value - that is a message that does not engender repentance toward obedience and righteousness, but rather loaded with earthly nectar or sugar-coated to please or deceive people; or any presentation that is not wholesome (nothing but the truth/word of Christ), but partial in nature; or any citation of the scripture in part, devoid of the "If factor" is a lie. As it is written; "I have not written to you because you do not know the truth, but because you know it, and that no lie is of the truth" (1 John 2:21). Whoever preaches, practices or encourages any gospel or doctrine contrary to the wholesome word of Christ is an anti-christ. "Who is a liar but he who denies that Jesus is the Christ? He is the anti-christ who denies the Father and the Son" (1 John 2:22). Again, "For we can do nothing against the truth, but for the truth" (2 Cor. 13:8).

This then is our statement of faith and belief: Jesus Christ is the truth, the way, and the life; there is no other author of salvation for mankind and none greater will ever come; He is the Word that abides forever (see John 1:1-5, 14:6; Acts 4:11-12; Heb. 1:1-3, 5:8-9; 1 Pet. 1:25). But Jesus Christ is the author of salvation to only those who implicitly obey all He has commanded them to observe to do (see Heb. 5:9). It is noteworthy that He became the author of salvation after He was found to be obedient to the end; for "though He was a son, yet He learned obedience by the things which He suffered "And having been perfected, He became the author of eternal salvation to all who obey Him" (Heb. 5:8, 9). And we know who said that whoever is not wholly/fully with Him is against Him (see Matt. 12:30)!

Whoever then professes Him but does not present and live His wholesome word, is a liar – for cursed is anyone who adds or subtracts from His word of life, or interprets or encourages others to interpret the scripture according to the customs and traditions of men (see Deut. 4:2; Prov. 30:6; Rev. 22:18-19). Whoever distorts, dilutes, subverts, suppresses or uses the word of God deceptively, or unwholesomely, or unfaithfully, lies and sins against the Holy Spirit. As stated inter alia, Jesus Christ is that cornerstone of eternal foundation. "For no other foundation, can anyone lay than that which is laid, which is Jesus Christ" (1 Cor. 3:11). Whoever surrenders and humbly falls on this foundation of rock shall be broken, and the Lord will mold and make him new and whole; but whomsoever this rock falls on, it would have been better he was never born (see Matt. 21:42, 44). Those who break the word of God with impunity and teach others to do so are anti-christs, who cause great offenses against God and His children (see Matt. 5:19, 18:6-7; Rom. 1:18; 1 John 2:18, 22, 4:13; 2 John 1:7)). The scripture divinely says that nothing can be done against the truth and no lie, no matter how sugar-coated will ever be of the truth (See 2 Cor. 13:8; 1 John 2:21). Therefore, whoever does not preach and abide in the undiluted word of Christ is not of Him (see 2 John 1:9-11).

The New Testament is filled with numerous warnings concerning false prophets and proliferation of lawless ones who would suppress the truth in unrighteousness. The Lord Jesus admonished us thus: "Beware of false prophets, who come to you in sheep's clothing, but inwardly they are ravenous wolves" (Matt. 7:15). The Lord further warned us strenuously to always beware of anti-christs, who would appear as His servants with such lying wonders – capable of deceiving the very elect of God (see Matt. 24:24). In his second epistle to the Thessalonians, the apostle Paul warned concerning anti-christs, thus: "For the mystery of lawlessness is already at work; only He who now restrains will do so until He is taken out of the way. And then the lawless one will be revealed, whom the Lord will consume with the breath of His mouth and destroy with the brightness of His coming. The coming of the lawless one is according to the working of Satan, with all power, signs, and lying wonders, and with all unrighteous deception among those who perish, because they did not receive the love of the truth, that they might be saved. And for this reason, God will send them strong delusion, that they should believe the lie, that they all may be condemned who did not believe the truth but had pleasure in unrighteousness" (2 Thess. 2:7-12).

Prudence, I believe, dictates that we pause to understand the above scripture. This world is now filled with millions of agents of the devil (false prophets, teachers, preachers, pastors, bishops, etc.) who hawk and display their power of darkness, signs and lying wonders to catch anyone with itching ears. And these things they do, because they are the most effective deceptive and manipulative devices to garner numbers for their pockets. Signs and wonders are the easiest ways to gain notoriety and wealth among the gullible – the things which empty "feel good," prosperity preachers and false prophets aim for – not eternal life, but personal (fleshly) satisfaction anchored on covetousness. As the apostle Peter stated: "But there were also false prophets among the people, even as there will be false teachers among you, who will secretly bring in destructive heresies, even denying the Lord who bought them and bring upon themselves swift destruction. And many will follow their destructive ways, because of whom the way of truth will be blasphemed. By covetousness they will exploit you with deceptive words; for a long time their judgment has not been idle, and their destruction does not slumber" (2 Pet. 2:1-3). Describing further the evil of false prophets, he (Peter) referred to them as "wells without water," who specialize in making empty promises of earthly vanity, while they themselves are slaves of corruption and hypocrisy (see 2 Pet. 2:17-19). The apostle Paul equally warned the Colossians of the inherent dangers posed by these false prophets and teachers, who present swelling words of empty deceit, according to the basic wisdom, tradition, and principles of the world (see Col. 2:8).

Let us now go back to our test scripture above (2 Thess. 2:7-12), that scripture which refers to those deceived by satanic signs and wonders of false prophets, as those who "perish," because they turned away from the truth of the gospel and doctrine of Jesus Christ. Although these deceived people know or should have known the truth by abiding in the explicit words of our Lord, yet they deliberately invite, partake or share fellowship with deceivers. The scripture states that those who have turned away from the undiluted and uncompromising truth of Jesus Christ are already condemned since there remains no more excuse (see John 3:19, 15:22; Heb. 6:4-6, 10:26-29).

Let me state boldly that signs and wonders are not for believers to seek, but rather for unbelievers to believe. The Lord said that it is a wicked and perverse generation which seeks signs, but none should be given it except the sign of Jonah, who was in the belly of a whale for three days. In other words, our sign is Jesus Christ, who died and rose again on the third day. So, those who seek after signs have no understanding that our sign (the Savior) has already come. Our sign is Jesus Christ, who came, died and rose for our salvation – the only remaining sign is His coming, which all those desirous of Him must make themselves ever ready, by living lives always pleasing, to Him to the end. As it is written: "Who then is a faithful and wise servant, whom his master made ruler over his household, to give them food in due season? Blessed is that servant whom his master, when he comes, will find so doing" (Matt. 24:45-46). A true believer/Christian (one truly born again) does not seek signs and wonders, rather signs and wonders follow him because he is god and the kingdom/Spirit of God is within him (see Mark 16:16-18). One who seeks signs to believe is yet to believe in Him.

Again, this I say, consistent with the word of God, those who run after false prophets and teachers, or have fellowship with them, share in their iniquity as well their reward. The time is now when both the deceiver and deceived shall be punished. As unfair as this may sound, we must carefully take heed that the law of accomplice applies with God. The one who fuels the flame of deception or manipulation, like the one who buys stolen property from a known thief is equally guilty of the crime in question. As it is written: "Where there is no wood, the fire goes out" (Prov. 26:20). Where there are no demanding itching ears, supply of falsehood, deception, manipulation and lying wonders dies. Once one is made privy of a matter of God's truth, he assumes a risk against his own interest, of being punished along with the deceiver on the same matter. Consistent with this position, God didn't hesitate to punish Adam and Eve along with the serpent which deceived them (see Gen. 3:14-

19). The Book of Jeremiah carefully documented God's wrath and punishment against false prophets and all those who listened to them (see Jer. 14:14-16, 23:30-34). The Lord Himself warned us to flee from false prophets, lest we perish with them (see Matt. 24:24-26); the apostle Paul admonished us to withdraw from unwholesome preachers, churches, and neither have fellowship with their unfruitful works (see Eph. 5:1-17; 1 Tim. 6:3-5; 2 Tim. 3:1-5).

The apostle John put the final nail on the matter in his second epistle, thus: "Whoever transgresses and does not abide in the doctrine of Christ does not have God. He who abides in the doctrine of Christ has both the Father and the Son. If anyone comes to you and does not bring this doctrine, do not receive him into your house nor greet him; for he who greets him shares in his evil deeds" (2 John 1:9-11).

Let us turn to the next chapter for a simple definition and clarification of who is a true servant/disciple of Jesus Christ.

CHAPTER FIFTEEN

A TRUE SERVANT/DISCIPLE OF GOD

With the proliferation of millions of churches and people who profess to be servants of the Highest God, it has become a daunting task to identify who is a true servant of Jesus Christ – for many I tell you profess Him with their mouths, but in their deeds, they deny and blaspheme His name (see Matt. 7:21-23, 15:8-9; Rom. 2:24; Titus 1:16). He is a true servant of Christ who implicitly abides in His word, and His word abides in him – spiritually fused together in one accord with Him, as He is one with the Father (see John 8:31, 15:14). Whoever implicitly obeys all He has commanded to do is the one who abides in Him. "Now he who keeps His commandments abides in Him, and He in him. And by this, we know that He abides in us, by the Spirit whom He has given us" (1 John 3:24). This I say then without reservation: whoever teaches, preaches, practices or encourages others to practice any word, gospel or doctrine contrary to the wholesome, undiluted and uncompromising truth of Christ is not of Him. In truth, the person hates Christ (See Matt. 12:30; John 14:15, 23, 24). A servant cannot preach, act or practice contrary to his master. The Lord chose His apostles for two reasons – to be with Him, that is, to be as He is, totally transformed into His image – for two cannot walk together without complete agreement, and one cannot preach or teach what he does not know; and fulfil His mandate/commission – which is to bear fruits that remain (see Matt. 28:19, 20; Mark 3:14; John 15:16).

ROLE OF A PROPHET/SERVANT/MAN OF GOD

There is indeed one single most important role of a true servant of God – that is to turn God's people away from their evil or wicked ways and return them to God's undiluted truth or highway of righteousness and holiness – a duty to ensure that none perishes. In other words, the role of a true servant of God is to get His people to repent and return to God's only foundation of eternal life - fear of God, which is to depart from all evil/sinful deeds (see Jer. 6:16; Matt 3:1-3, 8-10, 4:17. 28:19-20). The Spirit of God is upon a person whom God has anointed to preach His undiluted truth – not the servants of "feel good" or prosperity doctrine – but rather only God's word which is spirit and life (see Is. 61:1; John 6:63). A true servant of God is anointed to heal the broken hearted, not to devour them, to proclaim liberty to the captives, by teaching them to know the truth, not putting them into bondage; and to give sight to the blind, by removing the scales from their eyes, by the knowledge of the truth, not leading them to eternal blindness, for his covetous gain (see Is. 61:1-2; Luke 4:18-19). He is not a prophet of God who only tells people their names, addresses, telephone numbers, earthly things and evil spirits and imaginary enemies after their lives – for I suppose a magician can do all that. For what does the kingdom of God have in common with perishable things that are devoid of eternal value? He is a true prophet of God who allows God to use him to transform the heart of a sinner to the image of God. The greatest sign, wonder, miracle or healing is salvation – total transformation of a person to the image of Christ. This is the only purpose of our calling; it is the fulfillment of the whole duty of every person, and it is the only commission of Christ (see Eccl. 12:13; Matt. 28:19-20; John 3:3, 5, 6; Rom. 8:28-29). As it is written: "I have not sent these prophets, yet they ran. I have not spoken to them, yet they prophesied. But if they had stood in My counsel, and had caused My people to hear My words, then they would have turned them from their evil way and from the evil of their doings" (Jer. 23:21-22). The first ministration of all God's servants of the old and even our Lord Jesus Christ was urging people to repent of, and forsake their evil ways so that they would not perish. The only commission of the Lord to His servants is for them to go all over the earth and get people to repent and obey all He has commanded. Anything short of eternal life is fleshly, earthly, and perishable with using. As it is written: "For what profit is it to a man if he gains the whole world, and loses his own soul? Or what will a man give in exchange for his soul?" (Matt. 16:26). We are called to ensure that no single soul perishes - for that is the will of our God, and we know that only those who do His will are acceptable to Him.

Finally, I say to all, especially those who profess to be entrusted with the gospel and doctrine of Jesus Christ: cursed is he who deceives in the name of the Lord, or causes others to sin against Him; woe to him who is deceived, but cursed are both the deceiver and deceived, when the deceived knows or should have known the truth, yet he intentionally, knowingly, willingly or recklessly invites the deceiver; cursed is anyone who puts God's children into bondage; cursed is he who says the Lord has said when He has not said; cursed is the man who feeds himself by eating God's flock; blessed is the man who drinks His blood and eats His flesh rather than mere "pleading" the blood of Jesus; and cursed is he who adds to or subtracts from His word.

CHAPTER SIXTEEN

THE PHARISEES VERSUS THE PRESENT GENERATION PREACHERS

It is only fair I suppose, to examine a short comparison between the Pharisees of the Lord's time and the present generation of "feel good" and prosperity preachers. The Pharisees were bitterly rebuked by the Lord because they were hypocrites – because although they preached the truth handed down to them by Moses, as well as encouraged people to abide in said truth, but they themselves lived lives of deceit by not doing what they preached. In other words, as hypocrites, the Pharisees deceived themselves and not their listeners. As it is written "The scribes and the Pharisees sit in Moses' seat. Therefore, whatever they tell you to observe, that observe and do, but do not do according to their works; for they say, and do not do" Matt. 23:2-3). The

109

Pharisees did their works to be seen and admired by men, thereby deceiving themselves, since God saw their heart. But such hypocrisy so infuriated the Lord that He strongly admonished His disciples/servants thus: "For I say to you, that unless your righteousness exceeds the righteousness of the scribes and Pharisees, you will by no means enter the kingdom of heaven" (Matt. 5:20).

The instant question then is, who is worse – the Pharisees or the present generation of "feel good" prosperity and covetous preachers? It is certainly evident that the latter is the worst enemy of the kingdom of God, because of the level of violence it has perpetuated against God. A hypocrite is a victim of himself – he wallows up in self-deceit – being a danger to his own soul. The Pharisees preached and encouraged undiluted word as commanded by Moses – they never added to, or subtracted from it, neither did they handle it deceptively or unfaithfully, for covetous gain. A mere imagination of the prevailing abominable heresies being preached, practiced and encouraged by present agents of darkness is sufficient to send a shock to the spine of those who truly love God. Most who profess to be servants of Jesus Christ deny Him out rightly by either preaching and practicing their own gospel and doctrine, or presenting unwholesome and diluted word of Christ, while perfecting their "psychology 101" feel good, prosperity and demonic gospel and doctrine (see 1 Tim. 6:3-10; 4:1-2; 2 Tim. 4:1-5; Titus 1:16; 2 Pet. 2:16). They not only break the word of Christ, but they also would not stop until they teach others to do the same, thereby putting them in disobedience and bondage. As it is written: "Whoever therefore breaks one of the least of these commandments, and teaches men so, shall be called least in the kingdom of heaven; but whoever does and teaches them, he shall be called great in the kingdom of heaven" (Matt. 5:19).

The Pharisees caused lesser damage to the kingdom of heaven than the present generation of preachers, in that they deceived themselves – thereby being innocent of anyone's blood on their heads. Unlike the present generation of manipulators, deceivers and covetous "feel good" and prosperity liars who have not only opted for the destructive path but are determined to take all who come to them to the same path – through the breaking of the law and teaching and encouraging others to do the same. They preach and encourage worthless "feel good" and prosperity doctrine which only leads to earthly gratification and death. As it is written in the first epistle of the apostle John; "Do not love the world or the things in the world. If anyone loves the world, the love of the Father is not in him. For all that is in the world—the lust of the flesh, the lust of the eyes, and the pride of life—is not of the Father but is of the world. And the world is passing away, and the lust of it; but he who does the will of God abides forever. Little children, it is the last hour; and as you have heard that the Antichrist is coming, even now many antichrists have come, by which we know that it is the last hour" (1 John 2:15-18). Whoever does the will of God abides forever – God's ultimate desire/will is that no one should perish, but has eternal (everlasting) life with Him – and His will for His servants is to fulfil the purpose of their calling through implicit obedience, and getting others to turn away from all evil deeds and return to His undiluted truth (see Ezek. 18:23; Matt. 7:21-23: 28:19-20: John 3:16). As the Apostle Paul strongly warned the Colossians: "Beware lest anyone cheat you through philosophy and empty deceit, according to the tradition of men, according to the basic principles of the world, and not according to Christ (Col. 2:8). The apostle Peter was on point in his characterization of "feel good" and prosperity preachers: "…They are spots and blemishes, carousing in their own deceptions while they feast with you, having eyes full of adultery and that cannot cease from sin, enticing unstable souls. They have a heart trained in covetous practices, and are accursed children". "These are wells without water, clouds carried by a tempest, for whom is reserved the blackness of darkness forever. For when they speak great swelling words of emptiness, they allure through the lusts of the flesh, through lewdness, the ones who have actually escaped from those who live in error. While they promise them liberty, they themselves are slaves of corruption; for by whom a person is overcome, by him also he is brought into bondage" (2 Pet. 2:13-14, 17-19).

It is not enough to preach the word of God – for it is required of one who preaches it to live it completely. Whoever preaches the word of God, which word is sharper than a two-edged sword, must be careful to present it completely and faithfully, as well as live by it, or die by it. A teacher can certainly not teach what he does not know, and the only way to know the word of God is to eat, drink, breath and live it, without any shadow of compromise. But the one who deliberately and unfaithfully presents the word partially – presenting only the sugar-coated (sweet, feel good, prosperity, blessings) aspect of the word of God commits abominable heresy as an antichrist. Whoever humbly falls on this word shall be saved, but whoever this word falls on, will be destroyed (See Jer. 23:28-29; Matt. 21:44; Rev. 22:18-19).

THE FIVE INDICTMENTS

There are five indictments against all of us who preach or serve the Lord, lest we dare serve Him without fear and rejoice without trembling at His word. It is my considered belief and conclusion that all Christians, irrespective of their church or denominational positions face these indictments.

a) We condemn ourselves if we do not live what we preach or teach. If what we do during the day is different from what we do at night, we condemn ourselves (see Matt. 12:36-37).

b) The wrath of God is on those who suppress the word of God in unrighteousness (feel good, prosperity, covetousness, using the word deceitfully or unfaithfully) (see Rom. 1:18-25).

c) We are counted least and unfit to enter His rest if we intentionally, knowingly, willingly or recklessly break the word of God and teach and encourage others to do so (see Matt. 5:19).

d) It would have been better if we were never born, than to cause any offense against vulnerable children of God, including taking undue advantage of them (see Matt. 18:6-14).

e) We are condemned already if we out rightly reject the truth – keep in mind that half-truth amounts to rejection of the whole truth (see John 3:19; 12:47-48; 1 John 2:21).

THE MYSTERY OF BARREN VERUS BAD TREE

Let me share with you the mystery of a barren and a bad tree, which is analogous to the Pharisees and the present generation of preachers. A barren tree/branch will be taken away or given some helping hand, peradventure it may become fertile (see Luke 13:6-9; John 15:1-2). Unlike the barren tree, a bad tree is cut down and cast into fire (see Matt. 7:19). Again, unlike the barren tree which if it is taken away, or even cut down, dies forever, a bad tree on the other hand, continues its evil deeds after it has been cut down and burnt. A bad tree bears many bad fruits, which are dispersed all over the globe, and you know what bad fruits do – they grow into bad trees which produce more of their own bad fruits. To get rid of a bad tree requires an almost impossible task of destroying the bad tree and all its bad fruits. A barren tree or branch is simply taken away by the Lord – meaning that there remains yet a chance or hope of being grafted in, if it repents and becomes productive.

This mystery comes alive as the apostle Paul, writing to the Romans concerning some Jews who were broken off due to unbelief, thus: "Therefore consider the goodness and severity of God: on those who fell, severity; but toward you, goodness, if you continue in His goodness, otherwise you also will be cut off. And they also, if they do not continue in unbelief, will be grafted in, for God is able to graft them in again" (Rom. 11:22-23).

The alarming and horrendous proliferation of bad trees and their fruits, and their abominable violence against the kingdom of God has almost eroded any trust and confidence in the body of Christ. The most dangerous enemy is the enemy within, whose activities make the name of the Lord evil spoken of, and unto them is fulfilled the Lord's parable of the enemy sowing tares among the wheat (see Matt. 13:24-30). Let us all heed the admonishment of apostle Paul: "Therefore, since we have this ministry, as we have received mercy, we do not lose heart. But we have renounced the hidden things of shame, not walking in craftiness nor handling the word of God deceitfully, but by the manifestation of the truth commending ourselves to every man's conscience in the sight of God" (2 Cor. 4:1-2).

May God use this piece to provoke all of us to repentance unto good works, and fulfillment of the purpose of our calling – which is to be good trees that bear good fruits that remain until the appearance of our Lord Jesus Christ. Amen.

CHAPTER SEVENTEEN

AVOID WORTHLESS RITUALS – DELIVERANCE & LIBERATION

Let me strongly warn all children of God to avoid, reject, shun and abhor worthless and demonic rituals which only increase idolatry and bondage. It is sad that one of the most lucrative, crafty, cunning, manipulative, deceptive and lying schemes of agents of darkness (especially in Africa), for covetous gain and cheap earthly fame is the proliferation of the so-called deliverance and liberation ministries, modeled after fetish and occultist practices. Alarmingly and shamelessly, these false prophets and pastors run in millions, aggressively parading and hawking their acquired demonic powers to deceive people into believing that such ritualistic and worthless exercises can set them free from spiritual attacks and other spiritual or physical ailments. These they do shamelessly while charging their victims hefty sums of money. As it is written: "The coming of the lawless one is according to the working of Satan, with all power, signs, and lying wonders, and with all unrighteous deception among those who perish, because they did not receive the love of the truth, that they might be saved" (2Thess 2:9-10). The Lord condemned the same practice by the Pharisees, thus: "Woe to you, scribes and Pharisees, hypocrites! For you devour widows' houses, and for a pretense make long prayers. Therefore, you will receive greater condemnation" (Matt 23:14).

This I state unequivocally, there is no deliverance or liberation but salvation, which is the knowledge of the truth; and furthermore, whoever charges money to do God's work is a thief and robber. There is no amount of deliverance or liberation rituals that can set anyone free, but the knowledge of the truth (see John 8:32). And what is the knowledge of the truth? The truth is God, and the knowledge of God is eternal life (see Prov. 9:10; John 17:3). The only way to know God is to implicitly abide in His word; that is, becoming His word, or being one with His word; for only those who abide in His word and His word abides in them are true disciples or children of God (see John 8:31;15:14; Rom. 8:14). For only the knowledge (knowing, doing and living) of the truth shall set one free; if any claims to know Him but does not keep all He has commanded for us to observe to do, he is a liar who deceives himself. As it is written: "Now by this, we know that we know Him if we keep His commandments. He who says, "I know Him," and does not keep His commandments, is a liar, and the truth is not in him. But whoever keeps His word, truly the love of God is perfected in him. By this, we know that we are in Him" (1 John 2:3-5). Again, as stated above, he is a thief and robber who charges money for that which is freely given (see Matt. 10:8). But these false and deceptive deliverers and liberators prescribe doses of assorted and expensive food and huge sums of money to go to their victims' homes for one or more nights of worthless rituals, including but not limited to long repetitious hollering, excited utterances of mingled interest and horror and barbaric cutting down of valuable economic trees, where ostensibly some of the evil spirits that torment the victim or his family have secretly embedded themselves. Some specialize in unearthing the ground for buried evil objects planted by wicked enemies (mostly relations), who have tied up the person's or his family's fortune and prosperity, or to kill them. A liberation exercise is never complete without instilling enmity that will survive its destructive trail - the liberators/deliverers would tell their gullible victims that either their uncles, siblings, next door neighbors or even parents are after their lives and well-being. There has been hardly any false liberation performed by these agents of darkness that didn't kindle cyclical flames of enmity, bitterness, hatred and even outright war of relations or neighbors.

I have had occasions of counseling numerous victims of these scams, called deliverance and liberation, including some who had had deliverance performed on them on numerous times. And even today, I remain amazed how some people, including the very highly educated, could be so enslaved into subjecting and submitting themselves to many worthless deliverances and liberations. It is my considered opinion that a reasonably sane person would object and refuse a surgeon who has performed many worthless surgeries on him. Even sadly, some beautiful female victims who the agents made to believe that they were being chased by spiritual husbands (most likely marine and water spirits), had found themselves violated by these covetous and sexual predators. Now, where do I begin and end to write of the abominable practices of these agents who engage falsely and covetously in delivering and liberating others while they themselves are slaves of Satan.

I suppose you might have heard of this other astonishing twist and method to their deception and covetousness – these days, these agents are liberating the land. They charge villages, towns, and communities huge sums of money to liberate the land that was created by God from the beginning, even before man was created. If the land is defiled, it means the people have defiled themselves (see Lev. 18:24-28). Therefore, for the land to be healed by God, the people who defile it need to repent and turn away from their evil ways. As it is written: "if My people who are called by My name will humble themselves, and pray and seek My face, and turn from their wicked ways, then I will hear from heaven, and will forgive their sin and heal their land" (2 Chr. 7:14). It is the wickedness and evil doing of people that defile them and their land; the only way to deliver a person, or liberate a people, or land is to devote time to teach them the truth which is anchored and established on the foundation of eternal life – the fear of God – which is to depart from all evil deeds.

The fear of God is the beginning of deliverance and liberation – the fear of the Lord being the beginning of knowledge of the truth which sets the captive free. "The fear of the LORD is the beginning of knowledge, but fools despise wisdom and instruction" (Prov. 1:7). "The fear of the LORD is to hate evil; Pride and arrogance and the evil way and the perverse mouth I hate" (Prov. 8:13).

If therefore any of these deliverers or liberators is a true servant of God, let him go to these villages and towns and teach the people to fear God and repent of their wicked ways – that is the sole role of a servant of God. The Lord's commission to His servants is to go to all nations and people and teach them to repent and observe to do all He had commanded; and this duty is to be done without charge, so as not to hinder the gospel of Christ (see Jer. 23: 22; Matt. 10:8, 28:19, 20). As the Apostle Paul pointedly said: "For if I preach the gospel, I have nothing to boast of, for necessity is laid upon me; yes, woe is me if I do not preach the gospel! For if I do this willingly, I have a reward; but if against my will, I have been entrusted with a stewardship. What is my reward then? That when I preach the gospel, I may present the gospel of Christ without charge, that I may not abuse my authority in the gospel" (1Cor. 9:16-18). The calling of God is a service, not a job.

Now, if any of these agents of darkness is willing to forsake his covetous and deceptive ways and do what is recommended above, and if God permits, and peradventure one soul truly turns to God and is transformed into His image, God may have mercy and save the community because of this righteous man. As it is written in the book of Jeremiah the prophet: "Run to and fro through the streets of Jerusalem; See now and know; and seek in her open places if you can find a man, if there is anyone who executes judgment, who seeks the truth, and I will pardon her" (Jer. 5:1). True deliverance/liberation occurs in the heart – involving circumcision of hearts. Therefore, without actual transformation of a heart – a heart of flesh replacing a heart of stone – there is no deliverance or liberation – for one must know the truth by living the truth, and the knowledge of the truth shall make him free. Hence the scripture defines salvation as a combination of true deliverance (fear of God leading to repentance) and transformation of the heart. "He has delivered us from the power of darkness and conveyed us into the kingdom of the Son of His love" (Col. 1:13). Therefore, true deliverance or liberation is salvation, period. One who needs deliverance is yet to be saved or born again of God's Spirit. The craze about ritualistic deliverance and liberation short of true salvation is mere deceptive ploy or scheme by manipulative and covetous elements to exploit and capitalize on the gullibility, vulnerability, and fear of those they are supposed to feed, encourage and set free by the knowledge of the truth. A true servant of God does all he does to God's exclusive glory; an anointed servant of God is to preach God's undiluted word; he operates within the scope and cause of his calling, to wit: to preach the word to the poor, not lie to them; it is to heal the brokenhearted, not to devour them; it is to proclaim liberty to the captives, not to put them in bondage for covetous gain and control; it is to proclaim the fear of God (depart from any and all evil deeds); it is to comfort and console all who mourn, not to abuse them under color of authority of priesthood/pastorhood; it is to give them beauty for ashes and oil of joy for mourning, not to charge them for worthless anointed oil of fear and bondage; it is giving them the garment of praise for the spirit of heaviness, not laying heavy burdens on their heads (see Is. 61:1-3). It was due to such abuses of the Pharisees that led to their condemnation by the Lord. As it is written; "For they bind heavy burdens, hard to bear, and lay them on men's shoulders; but they themselves will not move them with one of their fingers" (Matt. 23:4). Again, "But woe to you, scribes and Pharisees, hypocrites! For you shut up the kingdom of heaven against men; for you neither go in yourselves nor do you allow those who are entering to go in" (Matt. 23:13).

A servant of the Lord is supposed to feed God's flock, not eat or devour them, for God will require His flock from him. As it is written in the book of Ezekiel the prophet; "Son of man, prophesy against the shepherds of Israel, prophesy and say to them, 'Thus says the Lord GOD to the shepherds: "Woe to the shepherds of Israel who feed themselves! Should not the shepherds feed the flocks? You eat the fat and clothe yourselves with the wool; you slaughter the fatlings, but you do not feed the flock" (Ezek. 34:2-3). This then is an urgent appeal to all "feel good," prosperity, deceivers, and manipulators to repent today and turn away from their evil ways. For the day, will certainly come when all who profess to be servants of Christ shall render their account of stewardship before the Lord; and we know it is terrible to fall into God's hands of vengeance (see Ezek. 34:10; Heb. 10:30-31). For we know Him, who said; "Vengeance is Mine, and recompense; Their foot shall slip in due time; For the day of their calamity is at hand, and the things to come hasten upon them" (Deut. 32:35). Servants of the Lord are to preserve, not destroy God's vineyard; but hear now the lamentation of our God over the destruction of His vineyard by those who are supposed to preserve it. "Many pastors have destroyed my vineyard, they have trodden my portion under foot, they have made my pleasant portion a desolate wilderness (Jer. 12:10). It is indeed better that one was never born than for him to deceive, devour and destroy the Lord's flock/vineyard under color of authority of priesthood/ pastor-hood. God has carefully set the Eli family as an example of what He does with those who exploit, extort and devour His sacrifice (vulnerable broken and contrite hearts). (see 1 Sam. 2:22-36; 3:11-14). As it is written: "Whoever causes one of these little ones who believe in Me to sin, it would be better for him if a millstone were hung around his neck, and he were drowned in the depth of the sea" (Matt 18:6).

Dr. Emeka O. Ozurumba

THE OTHER DESTROYER OF HIS VINEYARD – THE ACCOMPLICE

When the deceived or victim, who knows the truth or should have known the truth, yet intentionally, knowingly, willingly or recklessly invites the deceiver, he becomes a partaker with evil doers and receives the same punishment as an evil doer (see Jer. 5:30-31). It is generally accepted that one who sponsors a thief by sending, assisting or buying from him is equally a thief. Therefore, whoever knowingly, willingly, intentionally or recklessly gives or invites a false prophet shall receive a false prophet's reward. As it is written: "Where there is no wood, the fire goes out; and where there is no talebearer, strife ceases" (Prov. 26:20). This is true, as it is with the theory of demand and supply. Supply dwindles when demand decreases. So, while these servants of darkness are justifiably condemned, those who invite, support, sponsor, encourage, and tolerate them are condemned with them. As it is written; "Whoever transgresses and does not abide in the doctrine of Christ does not have God. He who abides in the doctrine of Christ has both the Father and the Son. If anyone comes to you and does not bring this doctrine, do not receive him into your house nor greet him; for he who greets him shares in his evil deeds" (2 John 1:9-11). For all who reject the truth are already condemned (see John 3:19). And those who know the truth or should have known the truth, but decide to stray away from it, while joining or inviting deceivers, suffer the delusion from God (see Rom. 1:17-24; 2 Thess. 2:7-11). That is the reason the scriptures seriously warn us to flee from such false prophets/preachers/teachers, churches and denominations, where the wholesome truth is not presented and practiced in its entirety (see Matt. 24:23-26; Eph. 5:1-17; 1 Tim. 6:3-5).

CHAPTER EIGHTEEN

THE MYSTERY OF MYSTERIES – OVERCOMING SPIRITUAL FEAR AND OVERWHELMING 'GIANTS.'

As I have already stated above, a true child of God – born of His Spirit and transformed wholly into His image, is a replica of God. Anyone born of His Spirit is a spirit, with the necessary spiritual characteristics (spiritual heart, mind, body and a new spirit). As it is written: "That which is born of the flesh is flesh, and that which is born of the Spirit is spirit" (John 3:6). For one born of God is god to the world, even to the devil, having put on the new person who is created according to the image of God; "…and that you put on the new man which was created according to God, in true righteousness and holiness" (Eph. 4:24). Our Lord made it abundantly clear, as it is so true, that in this world, afflictions, tribulations, trials of all sorts abound, but nevertheless, He has overcome the world for us. Who is he then who overcomes the world, but he who overcomes the world in, and with Him; that is one who abides in Him, and His word abides in him – that is one who is one with Him – for all purposes. It then means that for one to overcome the world, he must necessarily be aligned completely and fully with God, (fused together) in strict accordance with His prescribed rule or way of victorious living. As it is written: "I am the vine, you are the branches. He who abides in Me, and I in him, bears much fruit; for without Me you can do nothing. If anyone does not abide in Me, he is cast out as a branch and is withered; and they gather them and throw them into the fire, and they are burned." (John 15:5-6)

As it is in a race, it is not enough to run to the end; but for one to overcome, he must of a necessity run to the end according to the prescribed rules of the race. Whoever wants to overcome spiritual fear or overwhelming burdens, must not only run to God, but he must do so as He has prescribed. This conclusion is consistent with our Lord's words: "…If anyone desires to come after Me, let him deny himself, and take up his cross daily, and follow Me" (Luke 9:23). The apostle Paul, writing to Timothy, did not mince any words in reminding him of this obvious truth, thus: "You, therefore, must endure hardship as a good soldier of Jesus Christ. No one engaged in warfare entangles himself with the affairs of this life, so that he may please him who enlisted him as a soldier. And also if anyone competes in athletics, he is not crowned unless he competes according to the rules" (2 Tim. 2:3-5).

It, therefore, behooves us to get an understanding of this truth – those who are of Christ must walk as He walked (see 1 John 2:6); and overcome as he overcame. "To him who overcomes I will grant to sit with Me on My throne, as I also overcame and sat down with My Father on His throne" (Rev. 3:21).

The million-dollar question is how do we become one with Him as to overcome spiritual fear? This is of crucial importance since one who is spiritually fearful is imperfect in love, meaning that the person is not right or perfect in God since God is love (see 1 John 4:7, 18). It, therefore, holds true that it is only by the perfection of love for God and all people that one can be freed of spiritual fear of the unknown. And as we can safely take spiritual notice of the fact that love is perfected by implicit obedience to every word of God, it therefore holds true that spiritual fear of the unknown is overcome by God's inseparable two keys of His kingdom – love, and obedience. As it is written: "If you love Me, keep My commandments." (John 14:15) Again, "…If anyone loves Me, he will keep My word; and My Father will love him, and We will come to him and make Our home with him" (John 14:23). Simply put, those who hate Him disobey Him. As harsh as the above statement may appear to be, nevertheless, it is biblically correct; for we know Him who said: "He who does not love Me does not keep My words; and the word which you hear is not Mine but the Father's who sent Me" (John 14:24). And again: "He who is not with Me is against Me, and he who does not gather with Me scatters abroad" (Matt. 12:30). Being one with, or having an intimate fellowship with God, the Creator of all things, the King of kings and the Lord of lords, makes the ideal divine alliance, whereby God Himself stands in the gap and overcomes for you. This must be so since our weapons of warfare are mighty in God – so being one with God overcomes all forces of darkness.

For one to obtain such a divine alliance or an intimate fellowship with God, one must so seek it with all his or her heart. And how does one truly seek God enough to find Him? As it is written: "Seek the LORD while He may be found, call upon Him while He is near. Let the wicked forsake his way, And the unrighteous man his thoughts; Let him return to the LORD, And He will have mercy on him; And to our God, For He will abundantly pardon" (Is. 55:6-7). To seek God or begin an intimate fellowship with Him, which leads to total liberation from the bondage of fear, starts with laying a solid foundation of eternal life – the fear of God. The scripture tells us that whoever wants to have fellowship with God, let him begin by examining his ways, with sincere willingness to fear God by repenting and forsaking all his evil deeds or ways (see Hag. 1:3-7). Hence the scripture says that the beginning of wisdom, knowledge, and understanding of God is to fear Him - the fear of God is to depart from all evil deeds (see Prov. 1:7, 8:13, 9:10; Job

28:28). In other words, to begin a perfect walk (oneness) with God, we must cease our romance or fellowship with darkness – since darkness is fear breeding ground. Even more importantly is the fact that God does not, and will never, have fellowship with darkness; neither with anyone who is saddled or encumbered with unfruitful works of darkness. Apostle John writing in his first epistle states thus: "This is the message which we have heard from Him and declare to you, that God is light and in Him is no darkness at all. If we say that we have fellowship with Him, and walk in darkness, we lie and do not practice the truth. But if we walk in the light as He is in the light, we have fellowship with one another, and the blood of Jesus Christ His Son cleanses us from all sin" (1 John 1:5-7). Therefore, to begin any meaningful journey towards our freedom from fear, we must first take off all filthy garments that weigh us down, with a sincere vow never to go back to our vomit. This is that broken and contrite heart that God will not despise.

LAYING HOLD ON THE TWO KEYS TO ETERNAL LIFE

Now that the first enemy (we) has been taken care of, the scales having being removed from our eyes, it is time to lay hold on God's prescribed method and ways of overcoming the world and the fear of the unknown. To do this, it is necessarily prudent for us to carefully follow the examples set before us by the one who has overcome the world for us. The question is how did He overcome the world for Himself, giving us an example to follow?

LOVE: THE GREATEST COMMANDMENT / KEY:

First and foremost, we must love God with everything within us, making sure that nothing ever comes or takes preeminence before Him. We must love and seek to love Him with everything we have, only putting Him first and last - when we find Him, we must make sure we love and endure with Him to the end (see Deut. 6:5; Matt. 6:33, 13:44-46; Luke 14:26-35). Our God gave us an example of such love which gives all for the most desirable when He offered His only begotten Son for us (see John 3:16, 15:13).

The most problematic thing is our required love for fellow human beings. Ironically, most people believe they can love God devoid of loving all human beings, whom He created in His own image. In so doing, most of us ascribe more importance to our love for God. But love is love, and whoever does not love other people, even one person, does not love God, since God is love. Our Lord, Jesus Christ, commands us to be perfect in love as our heavenly Father is perfect in love, by loving as He loved us (see Matt. 5:48; John 13:34-35). This must necessarily sink in our hearts since only perfect love casts out spiritual fear (see 1 John 4:18). It is only when we love God with all we have and love all people as God loves us, can we then dare say we are perfect in love. Hence, our Lord commanded us to love all, including, and especially, our enemies. By loving our enemies as God loved us when we were rebellious to Him, we will be distinguished as true children of Him (see Matt. 5:45-47; Rom. 5:8). But if we act contrary to His commandments, we are none of His – but children of the devil - who comes to steal, kill and destroy. This Spirit of life (not death), was demonstrated by Christ when He sternly admonished His two disciples who urged Him to avenge a slight of a Samaritan village by calling fire from heaven to consume the village. "And when His disciples James and John saw this, they said, "Lord, do You want us to command fire to come down from heaven and consume them, just as Elijah did?" But He turned and rebuked them, and said, "You do not know what manner of spirit you are of. For the Son of Man did not come to destroy men's lives but to save them." And they went to another village" (Luke 9:54-56).

Our Lord perfected love by forgiving all, even His tormentors and those who crucified Him; and when He was reviled, he did not avenge or "return to sender," but rather committed all to the righteous Judge of all (see Luke 23:34; 1 Pet 2:19-23). In other words, our Lord never avenged, neither gave room to the devil. Therefore, whoever wants to be free from fear should never, never avenge for himself. Vengeance of any kind provokes God, and brings a cyclical saga of death – vengeance begets vengeance, until it consumes all (see Lev. 19:18; Deut. 32:35; 2 Sam. 2:26; Prov. 24:29; Ezek. 25:1-17; Matt. 5:38-42; Rom. 12:14-21; Gal. 5:15; 1 Thess. 5:15; 1 Pet. 3:9).

FORGIVENESS:

Love is imperfect without complete or total forgiveness of all those we have conveniently and bitterly imprisoned in our hardened hearts. We must forgive all, at all times, lest our God will not forgive us (see Matt. 6:14-15; Luke 6:37). Moreover, we risk the chance of God retracting His forgiveness, if we refuse to forgive all who have wronged us (see Matt. 18:32-35).

It is the totality of the above love package that led the apostle Paul to conclude in his epistle to the Colossians thus; "But above all these things, put on love, which is the bond of perfection" (Col. 3:14).

IMPLICIT OBEDIENCE – THE SECOND KEY OF THE KINGDOM

Once we are successfully clothed with the garment of perfect love, then the next is to lay hold on the word of God, by implicitly living it. Again, our Lord and Savior, Jesus Christ set the example for us to emulate. When He was confronted with the devil's trials, He firmly laid hold on the word of God, by relying on it and referring the devil to it (see Matt. 4:1-11). One thing that our Lord never did was to give room to confusing, lying, manipulative, deceptive voices. He listened and obeyed only the Father's voice – He never allowed itching ears to develop. He just did every word of God, by living it. He ensured He maintained absolute fellowship with the Father always. As it is written: "And He who sent Me is with Me. The Father has not left Me alone, for I always do those things that please Him" (John 8:29). Let us pause momentarily to think about the above-cited scripture. The Son of the living God, God Himself, said that the reason the Father never left Him was because He (Christ) always did His Father's will, by way of implicit obedience. In other words, the Father would have undoubtedly left Him alone if He (Christ) chose to disobey the Father. Hence, He kept strictly to the Father's will and obeyed all His commandments (see John 5:19, 30-31, 6:38, 8:28, 14:31, 17:4). Having made Himself one always with the Father, He overcame the world and made Satan bow before Him. He never feared the devil because the devil, as the prince of the world had nothing in Him (see John 14:30). The prince or ruler of the world is also the prince of fear; and whoever has something of him (sin) in him, will never be free from the bondage of spiritual fear, until the shackle of bondage/sin is destroyed. A sinner is a slave of the father of liars and sinners (the devil).

It is noteworthy that our Lord, when He was tempted in the wilderness, successfully rebuffed the devil with the undiluted word of God, because He was the word, and He was the word because He lived the word. Unfortunately, the manipulators of the word of God who are devoid of spiritual understanding would ask their victims to declare or prophesy the word or simply endorse the word with resounding "AMEN," all in futility. As a teacher cannot teach what he does not know, so also one cannot declare or prophesy what he does not have. For we are privy to the fate of the seven sons of Sceva in the Acts of the Apostles (see Acts19:13-17).

It is evidently clear that without laying hold on eternal life, one will never be free of fear. God's most important desire is for His children not to perish, and to have understanding that if one gets life in Him – that which is imperishable and eternal – all other things are his and subject to him (see Matt. 6:33). One who has eternal life in him has God / kingdom of God within him; it holds true then that –behold all things of God are his, and all things of the earth, including principalities, are subject to him. It is when God is with us – Emmanuel – the mystery of all mysteries – that we can burst out in praise, singing – "Because He lives…". If that be our case, who then can harm us if God be with us; and who can stand against, or resist our God? (see Rom. 8:31; 1 Pet. 3:12-13).

OUR CASE STUDY: JOSHUA 1:5-8

The most potent weapon of the devil is fear; hence his agents are proficient and prolific fear tappers, hawkers, inducers, and initiators. It, therefore, means that we cannot overcome and cast out fear when we are afraid of the enemy. God knows the devil's tactics so very well that in all situations when He appeared to His people, the first two words He spoke were "fear not." God commanded Joshua to fear not, and be courageous, for no man or devil could stand him because as He was with Moses, He would be with him (Josh. 1:5). But only that he (Joshua) should ensure he fears not, and be courageous to observe to keep all God's commandments. In other words, if Joshua would adhere to keep God's commandments, against all opposition, or tribulations, or giants, or afflictions or battles, God would be with Him and fight the battles for him; and for that reason only, he (Joshua) would make his way successful and prosperous. As it is written: "Only be strong and very courageous [not because of the giants facing him], that you may observe to do according to all the law which Moses My servant commanded you; do not turn from it to the right hand or to the left, that you may prosper wherever you go. This Book of the Law shall not depart from your mouth, but you shall meditate on it day and night, that you may observe to do according to all that is written in it. For then [and only then] you will make your way prosperous, and then you will have good success" (Josh. 1:7-8). Finally, God told us again why Joshua should not entertain any fears other than the fear of God only: "Have I not commanded you? Be strong and of good courage; do not be afraid, nor be dismayed, for the LORD your God is with you wherever you go" (Josh. 1:9).

It is when we have done all that we are required to do and stand with Him in oneness, that we can burst out singing 'Because He lives in me and I live in Him.' But if He does not live in us, then what…? Let me serve this notice to all "feel good", prosperity gospel preachers and their deceived audience: God is with us when we are with Him; if we forsake Him, through disobedience, He will forsake us; and if we deny Him, He will deny us (see 2 Chr. 15:2; Matt. 10:32-

33; 2 Tim. 2:12). Let us therefore not walk in self-deceit, and deceit of others, in a false sense of security doctrine that nothing can separate us from the love of God when indeed our iniquities separate us from God (see Is. 59:1-2).

CHAPTER NINETEEN

UNDERSTANDING THE PLACE OF PRAYERS AND VIGILS

'**O**h, my people perish for lack of spiritual understanding. Oh, my people, who has blinded you that you should believe in lies? Alas, my people have 'prayed' and 'vigiled' out, for nothing, yet they refuse to repent and get an understanding of the truth of the mysteries of the kingdom of God. What is the purpose of these multitude and long daily prayers and vigils; and yet the land stinks with bloodshed, adultery, idolatry, robbery, runaway corruption, kidnappings, inhuman wickedness against one another, and murder, even in churches and places they have covetously set up to worship and defile themselves? Yet they pray and vigil every hour, calling on Him, whom they profess to be their God, yet they have not known Him the ordinance of righteousness and holiness. Thus says the Lord of Hosts, 'indeed, they call Me their God, but they lie, for in them is nothing of Me; they have rejected My rebuke and disdained all My counsel, gave deaf ears to numerous chances to mend their ways, and find pleasure in reproaching Me with their long and repetitious prayers and vigils, while their hardened evil and wicked hearts are far from Me; yet, even now, if these people will turn away from their foolish and wicked ways and get understanding, truly repent and obey My word, rather than make futile prayers and vigils to Me, I will hear from heaven; for I am a merciful God.'

While calling the children of Israel to repentance, the prophet Hosea, speaking as an oracle of God, lamented thus: "My people are destroyed for lack of knowledge [knowledge of the truth]. Because you have rejected knowledge, I also will reject you from being priest for Me; Because you have forgotten the law of your God, I also will forget your children" (Hos. 4:6). Again, the prophet Isiah wrote: "Therefore my people have gone into captivity because they have no knowledge; Their honorable men are famished, and their multitude dried up with thirst" (Is. 5:13). Writing in the Book of Proverbs, Solomon, the wise preacher, emphasized on the imperativeness of getting understanding with all we are getting, including wisdom, knowledge, and discretion. Yet, king Solomon in the exercise of the understanding God had given him said that wisdom is the principal thing (see Prov. 4:7). The question I have severally put to people is: which is greater, wisdom or understanding? So many believe that wisdom is more valuable than understanding, but they are wrong. Hence, the wise preacher said again: "When wisdom enters your heart, And knowledge is pleasant to your soul, Discretion will preserve you; Understanding will keep you, To deliver you from the way of evil, From the man who speaks perverse things, From those who leave the paths of uprightness To walk in the ways of darkness; Who rejoice in doing evil, And delight in the perversity of the wicked; Whose ways are crooked, And who are devious in their paths;" (Prov. 2:10-15). Affirming that wisdom or knowledge without understanding is dead, king Solomon reiterated the overriding importance of having understanding, thus: "Wisdom is the principal thing; Therefore get wisdom. And in all your getting, get understanding" (Prov. 4:7). Again, this is because, as he rightly said, God founded the earth by wisdom, but He established the heavens that are above the earth by understanding (see Prov. 3:19); and while through wisdom a house is built, it is only established by understanding (see Prov. 24:3); for wisdom only finds a home in the heart of one who has understanding (see Prov. 14:33). For example, while indeed it is a good exercise to live in a church, or clothe oneself with pompous titles, or recite the various scripture verses or pray or 'prophesy final'; it is only by implicit obedience of the word of God, which is understanding, that we can find acceptance in the sight of God (see Matt. 7:21-23). As Job rightly stated, "Behold, the fear of the Lord, that is [mere] wisdom, and to [actually] depart from evil is understanding" (Job 28:28).

Another example will bring this point home: It is mere wisdom to profess to love or know God, but it is only when we implicitly obey Him that we practicalize what we say. As the Lord said, "These people draw near to Me with their mouth and honor Me with their lips, but their heart is far from Me. And in vain they worship Me, teaching as doctrines the commandments of men" (Matt. 15:8-9). Again, "They profess to know God, but in works they deny Him, being abominable, disobedient, and disqualified for every good work" (Titus 1:16).

The merciful God, who has mercy on whom He will have mercy, that His purpose according to election might stand, has appointed His elect to eternal life, predestined them to be conformed to His Son's image, and given them two distinct powers – the right to become His children and to know (understand) the mysteries of His kingdom, which is within Him! (see Matt. 13:10-15; John 1:12; Acts 13:48; Rom. 8:29, 9:10-16). Without spiritual understanding of God's mysteries, we will continue to strive for vanity and grasp for the wind. It is indeed my considered conclusion that a Christian, devoid of spiritual understanding of God's mysteries is not only yet to be born of God (born again), but suffers double jeopardy – he is neither of the world nor of God (see Rev. 3:14-16). By way of definition, spiritual understanding can be said to be the practicalization or actualization of wisdom, knowledge, and discretion. Understanding helps us to set or shape our Godly priority – priority being the setting and management of all our affairs and time in strict order of importance and urgency/need. It

141

is this orderly setting and managing of our priority that keeps us from grasping for the wind, as well as keeps us from being deceived or deceiving ourselves, or opting for the easy and sweet feel good and prosperity gospel that leads to death. He who understands his way is never lost.

UNDERSTANDING THE PLACE OF PRAYER

For the avoidance of misunderstanding, let me say clearly that prayer is a very important part of a life of a child of God. For the sake of clarity and to dispel any misunderstanding of this very important matter, let me again say that it is very important and highly needed and expected of us to pray always. We are commanded to pray always and without ceasing so that we do not faint or lose hope. As it is written: "Then He spoke a parable to them, that men always ought to pray and not lose heart" (Luke 18:1). The apostle Paul urged the saints in Philippi to be anxious for nothing, but to make their requests to God by prayer (see Phil. 4:6). And to the Thessalonians, he wrote: "Pray without ceasing" (1 Thess. 5:17). However, we must pray with the understanding that prayer is not the key, but obedience is the key; and we do not receive because we pray, but because we keep His commandments.

THE PLACE/PURPOSE OF PRAYER

Our Lord Jesus Christ clearly stated the place and purpose of prayer or the reason why the children of God should always pray – to keep us from fainting and losing heart (see Luke 18:1). Again, our Lord admonished the three apostles (Peter, James, and John) for sleeping at the face of imminent danger rather than keep watch in prayer. "…, What! Could you not watch with Me one hour? Watch and pray that you enter not into temptation. The spirit indeed is willing, but the flesh is weak" (Matt. 26:40-41). The apostle Peter, in his first epistle, also said that the purpose of prayer is to cast all our cares or worries on Him; that is, we must believe and cast our hope on Him as our sole provider and deliverer, so that we can afford to be sober, vigilant ad keep guard over our soul, rather than faint and be distracted (see 1 Pet. 5:7-8). So then, we see that the purpose of prayer is to ensure that we maintain our watch, keep ourselves from tempting ourselves or being tempted by the enemy; prayer keeps hope alive so that we do not faint; we present our petition to God by prayer and supplication. For if we faint in a time of calamity or challenge, it means our faith or strength is small (see Prov. 24:10). But our faith or strength is anchored on obedience to His words. For we are made to understand the mystery of God, that faith comes by hearing His word; and he who has heard the word is the doer of the word, whereby, obedience to His words, that is good work which justifies faith (see Rom. 10:17, 2:13; James 2:14-24).

Having said that, let me quickly say also that prayer is neither the "master key," nor one of the keys of the kingdom, or to God's heart. This statement is true and worthy of acceptance: Prayer is not the greatest moving force that gets God to hear and grant our petition. Rather, the master key is implicit obedience to His commandments. If we abide in His word and His word abides in us, then we have justified confidence that not only He will answer when we pray or ask, but He will answer us before we pray. As it is written: "If you abide in Me, and My words abide in you, you will ask what you desire, and it shall be done for you" (John 15:7). And how do we abide in Him and His words abide in us? The apostle John gave us the answer in his first epistle: "Now he who keeps His commandments abides in Him, and He in him. And by this, we know that He abides in us, by the Spirit whom He has given us" (1 John 3:24). The prophet Isaiah emphasized on the benefit of being one with God by way of implicit obedience; "It shall come to pass That before they call, I will answer; And while they are still speaking, I will hear" (Is. 65:24). And why would God answer us before even we pray? Because we are His people and He is our God, and we are His people if we abide in Him and His words abide in us.

Let me state boldly and categorically that we do not receive (God does not answer us) because we pray, rather we receive because we obey and keep His commandments. As it is written in the first epistle of John, the apostle: "And whatever we ask we receive from Him, because we keep His commandments and do those things that are pleasing in His sight" (1 John 3:22). Let me sound a strong caveat! Whoever prays, let him pray according to the will and desire of God. And what is His will and desire? That we first understand and seek for that which is eternal, imperishable – eternal life with Him, which no matter what happens, we should never trade off with earthly things which all perish in time with using. This is the will and desire of God: that we fear Him (depart from all evil deeds) and implicitly obey Him – that it may be well with us and our families forever: "And now, Israel, what does the LORD your God require of you, but to fear the LORD your God, to walk in all His ways and to love Him, to serve the LORD your God with all your heart and with all your soul, and to keep the commandments of the LORD and His statutes which I command you today for your good?" (Deut. 10:12-13). Again: "Oh, that they had such a heart in them that they would fear Me and always keep all My commandments, that it might be well with them and with their children forever!" (Deut. 5:29). This ultimate will or desire of God was strongly emphasized by our Lord Jesus Christ when He urged us to focus on seeking first the kingdom of God and His righteousness if we desire for all other things (including answered prayers) to be added to us (see Matt. 6:33). "Now this is the confidence that we have in Him, that if we ask [pray] anything according to His will, He hears us" (1 John 5:14).

Let me state without any hesitation or reservation that although prayer (praying) is very important in our life, nevertheless, the least of all God's commandments, enumerated beatitudes and fruits of the Spirit are greater than it. Prayer is not among the commandments of God. As earlier stated, we do not necessarily receive from God because we pray, but rather because we obey and do those things pleasing to Him always (see 1 John 3:22). It is certainly true that I can apply or ask for admission or entitlement into a program, but I will only receive it if I qualify for it. This is so true and similar to court prayer – we can pray as passionately or loudly as we want for our desired relief from the court of law, yet we get what our facts establish or prove. Like the famous worship song of 'trust and obey' rather than love and obey – the two inseparable keys of His kingdom; our trusting and praying in disobedience is indeed grasping for the wind. Our Lord's prayer says it all (see Matthew 6:9-13).

PRAYER VERSUS OBEDIENCE

While prayer is a legitimate petition to God, the greatest prayer is implicit obedience. Obedience is one of the two keys of and to God's heart. Prayer without obedience is dead on arrival. Even the prayer of a sinner, except he prays with penitent (broken-heart – heart willing to forsake his evil ways) is not respected by God. As it is written: "Now we know that God does not hear sinners; but if anyone is a worshiper of God and does His will, He hears him" (John 9:31). While prayer gives conditional access to a privilege, implicit obedience gives one the right. One who only prays makes supplications/requests – begging and asking for mercy, grace, and favor from the owner; but one who obeys and does God's will is a joint-heir and therefore has a right to joint ownership with Christ – (and that is, with or without prayer). Such intimate relationship gives us the confidence and boldness to ascertain or access all things of our Father – making all things of our Father ours (see John 16:15, 17:10).

PRAYER OF THE REBELLIOUS AND DISOBEDIENT

God will not hear prayers of the wicked, sinful, rebellious and disobedient souls – they are insult and abomination to Him. Such rebellious souls may pray and vigil until kingdom comes, yet God will not hear (see Ps. 66:18; Prov. 1:24-33, 15:8). God regards such prayers and vigils as sacrifices of fools – abominations to Him (See Is. 1:10-20). And as for such fasting, including 'dry fasting'; and all the 'river', 'bush' and 'mountain' fasting and praying either by agents of darkness and deception or their victims, they provoke the anger of God; but obedience is His delight (see Is. 58:1-9). As it is written in the first book of Samuel, the prophet: "Has the LORD as great delight in burnt offerings and sacrifices [prayers], as in obeying the voice of the LORD? Behold, to obey is better than sacrifice, and to heed than the fat of rams. For rebellion is as the sin of witchcraft, and stubbornness is as iniquity and idolatry. Because you have rejected the word of the LORD, He also has rejected you from being king" (1 Sam. 15:22-23). Our Lord, Jesus Christ, strongly admonished us not to make futile prayers or sacrifices, thus: "Therefore if you bring your gift to the altar, and there remember that your brother has something against you, leave your gift there before the altar, and go your way. First, be reconciled to your brother, and then come and offer your gift" (Matt. 5:23-24). In other words, God will not answer the prayer of those with blood in their hands, including all those who engage in vengeful and dangerous prayers against their enemies, like 'Holy Ghost Fire', 'die by fire', 'drop dead and die', 'return to sender', etc. etc. Such prayers are an abomination to Him. If I may borrow from the apostle James: But someone will say to me, 'I am a prayer warrior, prayer is the master key, I fast and pray daily; and I will say to him, show me your prayer without obedience, and I will show you my prayer by my obedience.' Not surprisingly, I have been confronted with the argument that all we need do is to ask and we shall receive, knock and it shall be opened to us, and seek we shall find. Those who marshal out this argument lack spiritual understanding that the "thing" our Lord refers to is the Holy Spirit, not perishable earthly things (see Luke 11:9-13).

OBEDIENCE THAT EFFECTIVELY PRODUCES THE RIGHT RESULT

Obedience must be implicit for it to be spiritually sufficient and effective. Obedience to God's commandments or will is an all or nothing. As it is written by the apostle James: "For whoever shall keep the whole law, and yet stumble in one point, he is guilty of all" (James 2:10). Obedience must originate from a willing, and broken heart – not borne out of obligation or necessity. Most of us only remember to run to God when calamity strikes, and we suddenly become mighty prayer warriors. But I must say that battle readiness and planning takes precedence over unrehearsed reaction in the middle of a battle. Therefore, the best time to develop an intimate relationship with God and pray without ceasing is before calamity strikes. Then when trouble comes, we will have the confidence to pray and ask God to please have mercy and remember us. For imagine one attempting to get a loan from a bank with which he has no relationship or collateral, especially when the individual is a known convicted bank fraudster.

OUR CASE STUDY – ISAIAH 38:1-6

As we have read, King Hezekiah became sick, to the point of death. God sent Isaiah, His prophet to tell Hezekiah to put his affairs in order because his sickness will result in death. Hezekiah then turned and prayed (bitterly wept) to the Lord: "and said, "Remember now, O LORD, I pray, how I have walked before You in truth and with a loyal heart, and have done what is good in Your sight, " And Hezekiah wept bitterly" (Is. 38:3). And the Lord was so moved that He sent back Isaiah to Hezekiah, with this message: "Go and tell Hezekiah, 'Thus says the LORD, the God of David your father: "I have heard your prayer, I have seen your tears; surely I will add to your days fifteen years" (Is. 38:5). King Hezekiah didn't engage in unnecessary lengthy and futile babbling; rather he made his case of obedience to God, and

God remembered. May we get understanding by reading and accepting this piece, that God may remember us even before we pray. Amen.

CHAPTER TWENTY

FIGHTING A SUCCESSFUL SPIRITUAL WARFARE – ORDER OF SPIRITUAL WARFARE

This one thing is true and worthy of acceptance, a true child of God constantly wrestles against principalities and forces of darkness. So, remember, when the enemy comes like flood, do not begin to assume that you are alone or ask, "why me?", but rather be still and know that God will raise His standard for you, if truly you are one with Him. Because afflictions and trials are inevitable, the Lord admonishing His apostles, thus: "These things I have spoken to you, that in Me you may have peace. In the world, you will have tribulation, but be of good cheer, I have overcome the world" (John 16:33). The enemy specializes in the business of prowling around like a roaring lion, seeking for prey to devour (see Job 1:7; 1 Pet. 5:8). Wrestling with the enemy presents constant inconvenience, distraction, and possible derailment – unless we know and apply God's winning method/formula (warfare). There is one other certainty – no matter what the enemy throws at a true child of God, he does not, and will never have authority over his life. But there is a big "IF" – if the person is a true child of God, and one with Him, victory is assured him in the end, no matter how many principalities and forces of darkness wrestling against him. As it is written: "And I give them eternal life, and they shall never perish; neither shall anyone snatch them out of My hand. My Father, who has given them to Me, is greater than all; and no one is able to snatch them out of My Father's hand" (John 10:28-29). As the Apostle Peter said, "And who is he who will harm you if you become followers of what is good?" (1 Pet. 3:13). It, therefore, means that the only way to fight a successful/victorious battle against the devil is to make God our permanent ally – oneness with God, for all purposes.

HOW TO FIGHT A SUCCESSFUL SPIRITUAL WARFARE

Simply defined, a warfare is a hostile operation between enemies. Although I am a novice at military tactics and strategies, the many clues from the Holy Bible, have given me the needed confidence to present the order of successful spiritual warfare against the evil one, thanks to our Lord and

Savior, Jesus Christ, and the apostle Paul, who despite numerous odds, fought numerous successful spiritual battles during the course of their ministries. And now, armed with the writings of the apostle Paul on this issue, which carry more weight, since he fought and endured more spiritual and physical battles than the other apostles. As he wrote in his epistle to the Corinthians, he fought beasts at Ephesus, received forty stripes five times, was beaten with rods three times, was stoned once, suffered shipwreck three times, spent a night and a day in the deep, in perils of both the Gentiles, in the sea and wilderness, and among false brethren, in and out of prison in just about every city, endured more hunger and thirst, and endured a "thorn" in the flesh which he described as a "messenger of Satan to buffet me"; and although he besought the Lord thrice to take away the torn, the Lord answered him thus, "My grace is sufficient for you, for My strength is made perfect in weakness" (2 Cor. 12: 9). We ought to be encouraged by his (Paul) wonderful spiritual attitude toward numerous afflictions, which he referred to as "light affliction" (see 2 Cor. 4:17). From these useful and pertinent clues, I have managed to develop a set of orders of successful spiritual warfare, as follows:

THE FIRST ORDER – Understand the Nature of Our Warfare.

The scripture tells and reminds us that the battle is against principalities and forces of darkness – in a nutshell, evil spirits. As such, we must rule out any flesh and blood in this engagement, just as it is impossible for flesh and blood to enter the kingdom of God. As it is written: "For we do not wrestle against flesh and blood, but against principalities, against powers, against the rulers of the darkness of this age, against spiritual hosts of wickedness in the heavenly places" (Eph. 6:12). Therefore, we cannot war in the flesh, if we ever expect to be victorious against the enemy. "For though we walk in the flesh, we do not war according to the flesh" (2 Cor. 10:3). This leads to the obvious conclusion that spiritual warfare is a hostile operation against spiritual enemies (spirits). It is a battle between spirits; for only spirits understand themselves. For it is written: "For what man knows the things of a man except the spirit of the man which is in him? Even so, no one knows the things of God except the Spirit of God" (1 Cor. 2:11). Therefore, for us to execute a successful warfare against the devil, we must not only be spirits but of a higher Spirit of God. Hence, our Lord emphatically stressed that we ought to be born again and become gods, for us to enter God's rest (see John 3:5-6). Without this total rebirth or regeneration to His image, we can neither worship God in spirit and in truth nor can we withstand the onslaught of the devil (see John 4:24). Having clearly understood the nature of spiritual warfare, we will now turn to the second order.

THE SECOND ORDER – Knowledge of Self – Number One Enemy

Before engaging the enemy in a warfare, one must honestly take stock of his stand against his enemy – whether he is fit or not to embark on such engagement. This self-examination exercise requires absolute sincerity and honesty – for whoever deceives himself in the matter of this warfare will be killed, without remedy. This stage is the key to battle readiness, which in turn is the key to victory or vanquish. As the Lord admonished those who are desirous and willing to follow Him to count their costs, to wit: "Or what king, going to make war against another king, does not sit down first and consider whether he is able with ten thousand to meet him who comes against him with twenty thousand?" (Luke 14:31).

One must first consider his ways, whether he has sold himself to the enemy, that is, if he has given the enemy the right and authority over him, thereby weakening his defensive system or hedge. When under the attack of the enemy, a sincere and humble child of God should first and foremost examine himself, if he is in faith or one with God; he must consider his baggage which can weigh him down. As the apostle James wrote in his epistle: "Let no one say when he is tempted, "I am tempted by God"; for God cannot be tempted by evil, nor does He Himself tempt anyone. But each one is tempted when he is drawn away by his own desires and enticed. Then, when desire has conceived, it gives birth to sin; and sin, when it is full-grown, brings forth death" (James 1:13-15). Therefore, it is imperative that we walk our Christian walk by always considering our ways first, whether we are operating according to His perfect will (see Hag. 1:1-7; 2 Cor. 13:5).

OUR TWO CASE STUDIES ARE: JOSHUA THE HIGH PRIEST AND KING DAVID.

Joshua the High Priest and his filthy garment:

One cannot fight a successful warfare while clothed with filthy garments that mitigate against him. This baggage must go, for a new garment of warfare. Imagine God's high priest, Joshua, the one God plucked from the fire, standing, with the angel of the Most High and Satan had the audacity to stand at his right hand (not even the left hand) opposing him. And the reason it was so was because Joshua had filthy garments (heart) on, giving Satan a legitimate claim over him (see Zech. 3:1-3). Except the filthy garments were put off and replaced with rich clothes (God's armor), Joshua had no chance against the devil. "Then He [God] answered and spoke to those who stood before Him, saying, "Take away the filthy garments from him." And to him [Joshua] He said, "See, I have removed your iniquity [filthy garments] from you, and I will clothe you with rich robes [clothes]" (Zech.

3:4). It was after new clothes were put on Joshua that the angel of the Lord admonished him saying, "Thus says the LORD of hosts: 'If you will walk in My ways, And if you will keep My command, Then you shall also judge My house, And likewise have charge of My courts; I will give you places to walk Among these who stand here" (Zech. 3:7). In other words, if Joshua kept the way of the Lord, with no more filthy garments, nothing on earth can hinder him.

King David and the oversized armor of King Saul:

For one to successfully fight a spiritual battle, he must ensure that movement is not inhibited by excess baggage or oversized armor of men, or tradition of men, and not of God. Whoever allows himself to be bonded to man or man's tradition or religion, or reveres or adores men or puts his trust in men, or fears men, or gives glory to man, will not defeat the enemy. For man is just mere grass, wicked and untrustworthy in his ways (see Ps. 103:15; Is. 40:6; Jer. 17:5-9; 1 Pet. 1:24). David had to take off the borrowed armor of King Saul, and in its stead, he put on God's armor (armor of God – God's weapon of choice for him). "David fastened his sword to his armor [Saul's sword and armor] and tried to walk, for he had not tested them. And David said to Saul, "I cannot walk with these, for I have not tested them." So David took them off' (1 Sam. 17:39). David then took the armor and weapon God had used before to save him, and we know the outcome over Goliath, the giant. Hear David, "Then David said to the Philistine, "You come to me with a sword, with a spear, and with a javelin. But I come to you in the name of the LORD of hosts, the God of the armies of Israel, whom you have defied" (1 Sam. 17:45). It is noteworthy that David had to take off Saul's oversized armor in order to put on God's armor. Finally, David reminded us that to overcome the enemy, we must make the battle the Lord's battle; and this is impossible if we are not one with the Lord. Hear him again, "Then all this assembly shall know that the LORD does not save with sword and spear; for the battle is the LORD's, and He will give you into our hands" (1 Sam. 17:47).

Understanding the provisions of Second Corinthians Ten, Verses Three to Six

"For though we walk in the flesh, we do not war according to the flesh. For the weapons of our warfare are not carnal but mighty in God for pulling down strongholds, casting down arguments and every high thing that exalts itself against the knowledge of God, bringing every thought into captivity to the obedience of Christ, and being ready to punish all disobedience when your obedience is fulfilled" (2 Cor. 10:3-6).

The apostle Paul, writing in mystery, expatiated on our case studies by emphasizing that to make our weapons of warfare mighty against the devil, we must first take off all filthy garments (strongholds), and cast down acquired over-sized armor or baggage (all arguments and every high thing that exalts itself against the knowledge of God) that inhibit our movement/walk with God. Very unfortunately, most Christians, including ministers of the gospel, are ignorant of the mystery the apostle Paul wrote about in the above scripture verses. They believe or are taught wrongly that the apostle Paul was referring to the pulling down of the enemy's strongholds and casting down his arguments and every high thing that exalts itself against the knowledge of God. However, the apostle Paul meant that in order for us not to make our weapons of warfare of a canal nature but rather mighty in God, we must first and foremost rid ourselves of all strongholds (which include but not limited to our filthy garments, stronghold of men, false prophets, "feel good", prosperity, manipulative, deceptive and lying wonders of men) that mitigate against our soul (see 2 Cor. 10:4). Having done that, we must cast down all arguments and every high thing (pride, arrogance, stubbornness, complacency) that exalts itself against the knowledge of God. It is when we do this that we would be in a possible position to bring every thought (our thought, not the devil's) into captivity to the obedience of God (see 2 Cor. 10:5). It is then after we have perfected or fully fulfilled our obedience that we would be in a firm position to punish all disobedience, including that of the devil (see 2 Cor. 10:6). Now, let us pause to consider this matter again. How can we cast the devil's arguments and bring his every thought into captivity to the obedience of Christ? We know that Paul could not possibly mean that the devil would punish all disobedience (since he is the father of disobedience) after he has perfected his obedience of God, which is impossible for him to do. The apostle Paul told us how he was able to acquire the mighty weapons of warfare in God. "Therefore I run thus: not with uncertainty. Thus I fight: not as one who beats the air. But I discipline my body and bring it into subjection [subjection to the Spirit], lest, when I have preached to others, I myself should become disqualified" (1 Cor. 9:26-27).

THE THIRD ORDER – Knowledge of, and accurate intelligence about, the enemy.

Having honestly examined and assessed ourselves (the enemy within), the next order is to know and obtain accurate intelligence about the enemy without – the devil. For one to engage this enemy successfully, he must know him. We must thank God for providing all we need to know about the devil and his warfare tactics. All relevant and accurate information or intelligence about the devil is liberally x-rayed in the Holy Bible so that I need not write a volume here about him, who is the destroyer of good. It will suffice, I suppose, to mention a few characteristics and tactics of the devil. His strength is in his subtle and lying wonders and ability to project fears of different shapes and shades. As it is written, "Now the serpent was more cunning than any beast of the field which the LORD God had made. And he said to the woman, "Has God indeed said, 'You shall not eat of every tree of the garden'?" (Gen. 3:1). Notice that in his subtlety, he just tricked Eve into answering and wondering if God had forbidden them to eat of any tree, not just one tree. The same provoking and subtle approach he used against our Lord in the wilderness. Although he knew that Christ was the son of God, yet he chose the opportune season (when He was hungry), to move against Him by trying to provoke him either to question His identity or take matters into His own hands. Notice the devil's subtle and wicked style: "Now when the tempter came to Him, he said, "If You are the Son of God, command that these stones become bread" (Matt. 4:3). Mind you, if it were some of us, we would have boastfully and angrily shown the devil whom we are indeed, thereby succumbing to his tactics and obeying his voice; and whoever obeys the voice of the devil is his child or servant (see Rom. 6:16). A child or servant of God only obeys God's voice. "My sheep hear My voice, and I know them, and they follow Me" (John 10:27). "Yet they will by no means follow a stranger but will flee from him, for they do not know the voice of strangers" (John 10:5). Hence the Lord answered every trick of the devil with the undiluted word of God (see Matt. 4:1-11). We must pause to appreciate a clue for us – For one to fight a successful spiritual warfare, he must only heed the voice of God, not the devil and his agents.

From the two instances, which the devil portrayed his subtlety, it must be obvious to us that his primary objective is to get us to assume a rebellious self-dependence from our source. When this happens, as you can imagine, like a baby whose sole dependence on the nursing mother is severed, our naked vulnerability is exposed to all predators. The devil is unmatched in craftiness, cunningness, deceptiveness, manipulations, and lying wonders; being the chief liar and the father of it (see John 8:44). This then makes it necessary to align with the one who knows him best. The devil is also a parasite, and like all parasites, he oftentimes attacks without a willing host; therefore, this is always my prayer, "Father, lead me not into temptation, and restrain me from leading myself into temptation." As it takes two to tangle, let us heed the apostle James admonishment (see James 1:13-15). This enemy should be avoided and resisted at all cost since he only comes to steal, kill and destroy (see John 10:10). Whoever has fellowship with him has assumed his own certain death. The scripture tells us that the devil is the ruler of the world and its glory, and he can give to those who bow down and worship him; it holds true, therefore, that all those who are in love with the world, and all its glory, lusts, riches, and affections will not escape the snare of the devil (Rom. 8:5-8; 1 Tim. 6:6-10; James 4:4; 1 John 2:15-17). Let us make no mistake about this – this enemy is a persistently stubborn foe; he hardly gives up, he may be beaten several times, but he does not know how to give up. Fortunately, he appears to have a low I.Q. or limited intelligence in his repeated, and sometimes, childish tactics. He has no qualms about trying to derail anyone, even the Son of the Living God.

But our enemy has a major weakness: he hates the light and does not understand two potent weapons of our warfare – perfect love and implicit obedience. Now, that we know the enemy without, our simple equation is to eliminate the enemy within, as we turn to the fourth order of spiritual warfare.

THE FOURTH ORDER – Understanding and Assessing our Need.

Now that we seem to understand the nature of our warfare, and know ourselves and the enemy (devil), we must now determine our need – weapon of warfare and how to go about acquiring it. Since it is obvious that without God, we can do nothing, which means, on our own (flesh and blood) the devil being a spirit, will shred us to pieces if we dare fight him without a stronger ally. This calls for divine alliance, which is impossible without totally and unreservedly surrendering and submitting to God. We must acquire God's weapon of warfare by making an alliance with Him, before resisting the enemy. We must completely fulfill the terms of the alliance agreement laid down by our dominant ally – God. So, the condition precedent to the sealing of the alliance agreement is total and unreserved submission to God. As it is written: "Therefore submit to God. Resist the devil, and he will flee from you" (James 4:7). Simply put, if we seek and get the kingdom and God's righteousness first, all other needs, including God's hedge shall be added on to us (see Matt. 6:33). To fully understand the terms of the alliance agreement, we must understand and do what God requires of us - fear God (depart from all evil or sinful deeds), and implicitly obey all He has commanded us to observe to do (see Deut. 5:29, 10:12-13; Ecl.12:13).

Let us examine a case study relative to meeting the terms of the agreement. In the Book of Joshua, chapter one, God commanded Joshua to keep the terms of the alliance agreement if he wanted Him to be with him as He was with Moses; and if he would only do so, he should not be afraid of man or devil, for none would stand before him (see Joshua 1:5). The terms of the agreement are perfect fear of God (depart from all sinful/evil deeds), love, implicit obedience, and unreserved and total submission to God's will – being spiritually fused together in agreement with Him, who is the Creator of all things, including principalities (see Josh. 1: 7-8). Now that we have God, the Father of all spirits on our side, our next order is to wholly put on His armor over us.

THE FIFTH ORDER – Putting on and Maintaining God's whole armor.

Taking the whole armor of God is taking on His whole image – totally transformed to His image and following Him fully. It is being fused together spiritually with God; it is denying ourselves and taking the cross and following Christ daily; it is being a complete new creation in God, created as God in true righteousness and holiness (see Luke 9:23-25; John 3:3, 5-6, 15:7; Rom. 8:29; 2 Cor. 5:17; Gal. 3:27; Eph. 4:24). All those who are desirously determined to win this dangerous wrestling battle against the devil, must make haste to put on, and vow to maintain the whole armor of God. As it is written: "Therefore take up the whole armor of God, that you may be able to withstand in the evil day, and having done all, to stand. [maintain – stand firmly]" (Eph. 6:13). To maintain God's armor always, we must stand firmly rooted in the truth – be the truth by living it, which is implicit obedience leading to righteousness. In addition, we must take the shield of faith, which is justified and fulfilled by our obedience (good works) of every word of God, which is our salvation and sword of warfare against the enemy; and praying without ceasing, so that we do not faint and give room to the enemy to exploit our weakness (see Eph. 6:14-18). Now, let us look at our case study of putting the whole armor, as presented in the Book of Job, chapter one. The devil couldn't touch Job at all because Job had the whole armor of God (hedge) on him. It was God who made an impenetrable hedge around Job because Job was a just, blameless and righteous man – one who surrendered and unreservedly submitted all to God (see Job 1:1). We read that until God allowed the devil to touch Job, he (devil) had no power or authority over Job; as a matter of fact, he (devil) couldn't touch or stand before Job because of God's hedge around him. In other words, because of Job's alliance with God, God made Job god to the devil.

There is, of course, another good news, which should prompt us to quickly seek to put God's hedge or armor on us – a hedge around us also covers our household and all we have. Hear the Satan's response to God, "So Satan answered the LORD and said, "Does Job fear God for nothing? Have You not made a hedge around him, around his household, and around all that he has on every side? You have blessed the work of his hands, and his possessions have increased in the land" (Job 1:9-10). So then, what are we waiting for? The God we serve does not change; He remains the same, and there is no lie in Him. The greatest inheritance we can give our children is our total submission to God's will; and if we do so to the end, without looking back, God will never forget us and our families, no matter the afflictions of the present life. We will always be victorious against all wicked forces of darkness.

Finally, let me sound this note of warning. We cannot win this wrestling battle with fasting and praying alone, but with perfect fear of God, love and implicit obedience (see John 15:7; 1 John 3:22,24). Rather than plead the blood of Jesus, we must drink it – the blood (John 6:53-55); rather than worthless liberation and deliverance rituals, we must mend our ways – know and embrace the truth by living and being the truth (John 8:32, 36; 2 Cor. 3:17); rather than holding vigil to shout and scream at the devil and pray dangerous/vengeful prayers against our enemies, we should put away our wicked ways and love God and other people and implicitly obey Him; and rather than scheming for short cuts and painless and tranquilizing "feel good" pill, as alcoholics do, we should take the bitter Truth of the word of God, which is life and spirit (see John 6:63). For no sooner the alcoholic wakes from the influence of damaging hot drinks, he goes up to seek for more until it kills him. Taking hot drinks to an alcoholic is like making those who are deceived to feel good. Therefore, the scripture below is appropriate for all whose gullibility and itching ears have made them slaves of "feel good," and prosperity preachers. "Who has woe? Who has sorrow? Who has contentions? Who has complaints? Who has wounds without cause? Who has redness of eyes? Those who linger long at the wine, those who go in search of mixed wine. Do not look on the wine when it is red, when it sparkles in the cup, when it swirls around smoothly; at the last it bites like a serpent, and stings like a viper. Your eyes will see strange things, and your heart will utter perverse things. Yes, you will be like one who lies down in the midst of the sea, or like one who lies at the top of the mast, saying: "They have struck me, but I was not hurt; They have beaten me, but I did not feel it. When shall I awake, that I may seek another drink?" (Prov. 23:29-35). So, I urge all who are in manipulative, deceptive, covetous, and lying strongholds of men to flee today from their captors.

It is my humble and tearful prayer that our merciful God, who does not wish for any of His children to perish, uses this book to set His children free from the bondage of men and spiritual fear of the unknown, all to His exclusive glory.

"Therefore, as the Holy Spirit says, "Today, if you will hear His voice, do not harden your hearts, as in the rebellion…" (Heb. 3:7-8)

To God Almighty alone, the only Living God, be all the glory now and forever more. AMEN.